MUSIC

INVESTIGATE THE EVOLUTION OF AMERICAN SOUND

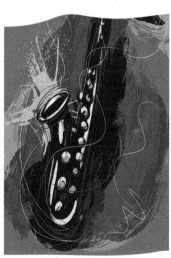

Donna Latham
Illustrated by
Bryan Stone

~ Titles in the *Inquire and Investigate* Series ~

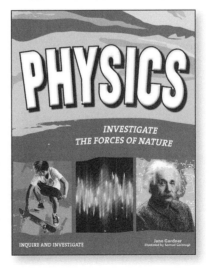

green
press
INITIATIVE

Nomad Press is committed to preserving ancient forests and natural resources. We elected to print *Music: Investigate the Evolution of American Sound* on Thor PCW containing 30% post consumer waste.

Nomad Press made this paper choice because our printer, Sheridan Books, is a member of Green Press Initiative, a nonprofit program dedicated to supporting authors, publishers, and suppliers in their efforts to reduce their use of fiber obtained from endangered forests.

For more information, visit **www.greenpressinitiative.org**.

Nomad Press
A division of Nomad Communications
10 9 8 7 6 5 4 3 2 1

This book was manufactured by Sheridan Books, Ann Arbor, MI USA.
November 2013, Job #352148
ISBN: 978-1-61930-199-3

Illustrations by Bryan Stone
Educational Consultant, Marla Conn

Questions regarding the ordering of this book should be addressed to

Nomad Press
2456 Christian St.
White River Junction, VT 05001
www.nomadpress.net

Contents ▶

Timeline........vi

Introduction
Make Your Own Kind of Music........1

Chapter 1
Good Vibrations........5

Chapter 2
Colonial Times and the Music of Slave Life........21

Chapter 3
The Birth of a New Nation: Patriotic Music........39

Chapter 4
The Roaring Twenties: Jazz, Blues, and Country........55

Chapter 5
War and Social Change: Patriotism and Protest........67

Chapter 6
Rock and Roll Is Here to Stay........85

Chapter 7
The Age of Technology........97

Glossary ▼ Resources ▼ Index

▾ TIMELINE

1607 ....Jamestown, Virginia, is settled by English colonists.

1619 ....African people are brought to Jamestown and sold into slavery. They share work songs and field hollers, relying on memory in the oral tradition.

1640 ....America's first book, The Bay Psalm Book is printed.

1700 ....Slaves sing songs based on old testament stories, reflecting their belief in Christianity.

1740 ....The Negro Act bans slaves from beating drums in South Carolina. They resist with the hand clapping and leg slapping of juba.

1775 ....The Revolutionary War begins. When British troops make fun of colonial fighters by singing "Yankee Doodle," Americans adopt it as their own.

1814 ....Francis Scott Key writes the poem "The Defense of Fort McHenry," which is renamed "The Star Spangled Banner." It later becomes America's national anthem.

1861 ....The Civil War begins. Julia Ward Howe writes "Battle Hymn of the Republic" after witnessing a skirmish.

1877 ....Thomas Edison invents the phonograph, a sound-recording device.

1913 ....*Billboard* magazine publishes a list of the most played vaudeville songs that are gaining popularity. This is a predecessor to their trademark Top 100 charts.

1917 ....America enters World War I. George M. Cohan composes "Over There."

1919 ....Chicago is established as the jazz capital with icons like Louis Armstrong performing in its clubs.

1923 ....The Charleston launches a national dance craze.

1925 ....Weekly radio broadcasts start at Grand Ole Opry in Nashville, Tennessee, featuring country and western music. Bessie Smith makes the first electronically recorded song "Cake Walking Babies."

1932 ....Vi-Vi Tone and Rickenbacker begin making and selling electric guitars.

1941 ....America enters WWII. People listen to the "Boogie Woogie Bugle Boy" on radios.

1945 ....American composer Aaron Copland wins the Pulitzer Prize in music for "Appalachian Spring," a ballet by Martha Graham that he composed in 1944.

1948 ....Long playing vinyl records are introduced by Columbia Records.

▾ AMERICA'S MUSICAL JOURNEY

1951 ....Jackie Brenston and his Delta Cats have the number one single on the *Billboard* R&B chart with "Rocket 88." Many consider "Rocket 88" as the first rock and roll record.

1954 ....Bill Haley and the Comets launch a frenzy with the huge hit "Rock Around the Clock." Elvis Presley becomes one of the first rock stars, with 60 million people watching him on the "Ed Sullivan Show."

1958 ....*Billboard* debuts its Hot 100 chart. Ricky Nelson's "Poor Little Fool" is the first No. 1 song.

1963 ....Bob Dylan popularizes protest songs. "Blowin' in the Wind" is sung at the March on Washington.

1964 ....The Beatles, a British band, gains popularity in America. This is the start of the "British Invasion."

1969 ....500,000 hippies and others swarm Woodstock for "Three Days of Peace, Love, and Music."

1973 ....DJ Kool Herc launches hip hop in the Bronx.

1979 ....The Sugar Hill Gang releases the first commercial rap hit "Rapper's Delight," popularizing hip hop nationwide.

1981 ....MTV debuts on August 1 with music videos geared toward adolescents.

1982 ....Michael Jackson releases "Thriller," the top-selling album in history.

1988 ....CDs outsell vinyl records for the first time.

2001 ....After 9/11 the current and former U.S. Presidents sing "Battle Hymn of the Republic" in the National Cathedral. America engages in war with Afghanistan.

2003 ....Apple iTunes Music Store is launched, allowing people to download songs for 99 cents.

2005 ....Pandora Radio, a web-based radio that personalizes its stations based on the listener's preferences, gains popularity.

2007 ....141 million iPods have been sold around the world.

2009 ....Pop icon Michael Jackson dies just before his comeback tour "This is It."

2010 ....Joan Baez sings "We Shall Overcome" for America's first African-American president, Barack Obama.

2012 ....The song "Gangnam Style" becomes the first YouTube video to surpass 1 billion views.

Introduction▶
Make Your Own Kind of Music

How does music inspire you?

 Music is an integral part of American history and heritage. It has the power to stir the soul and impact moods, to shape beliefs and motivate change.

MUSICAL NOTE

Use the Playlists throughout this book as take-off points for further exploration. They suggest songs, artists, and performances to listen to, view online, and download. If a QR code is provided, you can use a smartphone or tablet app to access the suggestion directly.

What's on your playlist? Perhaps your taste in music is eclectic, with pop artists, R&B bands, and classic rock all providing the backbeat for your life. Do you download hip-hop tracks as soon as they drop, or scout old-school brick-and-mortar record shops for vintage vinyl? Maybe you make your own kind of music, belting out show tunes on karaoke machines, playing with your garage band, or guitar jamming with apps.

Music is inspirational. Have you ever wondered what's behind the music that moves you? Have you thought about the inspiration behind a popular song, whether it's indie or Top 40? Musical tastes are often deeply personal. You might love hip-hop while your brother only listens to jazz. But looking at musical trends offers surprising insights into a collective identity. Artists create music that reflects the time in which they live, with all its joy, strife, and messiness.

Social, political, and religious influences have shaped American sound from before we were a nation to the present. This same music helped form and empower an American identity, one with common core values that champion the individual, embrace freedom and democracy, and fight for civil rights. Within that collective identity is also the cherished right to protest and speak up—or sing out—against injustice.

RICH MUSICAL DIVERSITY

With its wide diversity of people and backgrounds, it's not surprising that the United States boasts an amazing array of musical influences from all over the world. From its earliest settlers, Americans discovered ways to weave Old World European traditions with new cultural influences to compose a unique identity.

The United States has contributed greatly to the world music scene, creating genres considered distinctly American. Its musical journey traveled from hymns and folk songs to patriotic tunes that fostered unity in wartime. It leapt from field hollers and soared on the wings of spirituals urging forbearance and spreading hope to those living in slavery. American sound be-bopped through jazz and the blues and throbbed into the rhythm of rock and hip-hop. And it rocks on!

ART AND SCIENCE

Music is both an art and a science. It's a constantly evolving creative expression that evokes strong emotional responses. Musicians are continually inspired by artists of the past, even as they find ways to add their own spins and create works that are uniquely their own.

🎵 **There is a lot of new vocabulary in this book! Turn to the glossary in the back when you see a word you don't understand.**

BLAST FROM THE PAST

In 2006, the popular TV show *Lost* featured the song "Make Your Own Kind of Music" by Barry Mann and Cynthia Weil. It's a golden oldie that champions individualism and urges singing your own special song. "Make Your Own Kind of Music" was a 1969 Top-40 hit for alto Cass Elliot (1941–1974). From 1965 until 1968, "Mama" Cass performed with Rock and Roll Hall of Famers the Mamas and the Papas, whose beautiful folk-pop harmonies rose from the Southern California music scene. After the band's bitter break-up, Elliot enjoyed a solo career until her death at age 32.

♪ Evolving technology such as the phonograph, radio, iPod, and Internet have made music and its varied messages widely accessible.

In *Music: Investigate the Evolution of American Sound*, you'll explore and analyze the history behind this popular art form. The activities in the book will introduce you to the physics of sound, music, and dance, as well as the physiology of hearing and singing. Like artists of the past and present, you'll apply what you discover to craft your own instruments, kick up your heels, write lyrics, compose music, and put on a show.

Adam Levine of the band Maroon 5 told *Vanity Fair* magazine, "The diversity in people's tastes is so much cooler. Everyone is saying MP3s and the Internet have ruined the music business and it's sad there are no more record stores—but music is so present now in the culture. More than it's ever been. That's a result of the technological advancements we've made."

We're fortunate to live in a time when we can access songs, music videos, TV appearances, movie clips, and recorded performances, even those produced decades ago. You can do this anytime, anywhere, with just the touch of a fingertip or a search on YouTube.

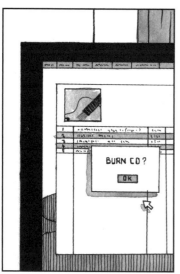

Chapter 1 ▶
Good
Vibrations

How do vibrations
create sound?

♫ Acoustics is the scientific study of sound, which is a form of energy.

You usually know right away whether something sounds good to you or not. If you like a song you keep listening, if not, you change the station. What exactly is sound and why do we hear it?

VIBRATIONS IN THE AIR

When an object vibrates, it moves molecules in the air. These molecules bump into each other to make a sound wave. When waves of sound energy move away from the source of the vibrations and travel through a medium such as metal, water, or air, it causes a sensation in the ear. That sensation is sound.

Pitch is how high or low a sound is. If the vibrations are fast, the pitch is high. If they are slow, the sound is low. You've probably heard the siren of an ambulance blast shrill, high-pitched sounds to demand your attention. But foghorns, with their low-pitched blares, get your attention too.

Loudness and intensity affect the vibrations of sound. When you feel the floor tremble under your feet during a rock concert or feel bleachers rumble as a marching band leads its school team onto the field, you're experiencing loud, intense sounds with huge amounts of energy.

The loudness of sound is measured in a unit called a decibel (dB). Decibels are the force of sound waves against the ear. As sounds grow louder, decibels increase. A typical conversational tone you might use when chatting with a friend measures approximately 65 dB. If you yell across a room to get another friend's attention, that level increases to about 95 dB. If you have to raise your voice for someone else to hear you, you're at 85 dB or more. Long or repeated exposure to sounds above 85 dB can cause hearing loss.

THE HUMAN EAR

Your ear is extremely sensitive. How does it work? The pinna is the external portion of the ear that you can see. It captures sound waves and channels them to the external auditory canal. Sound waves move deeper to reach the tympanic membrane, typically called the eardrum. In the eardrum, the energy of sound waves transforms into sound. As the vibrations hit the eardrum, it flexes inward and outward. Sound waves vibrate the eardrum back and forth as the sensitive membrane detects the movement of molecules. The eardrum vibrates at a speed identical to the vibrations of sound.

MUSICAL NOTE

The decibel scale starts at zero. That's the weakest audible sound. A sound above 130 dB or more, such as a jet engine at 100 feet (about 30 meters), causes actual pain in your ear. And 160 dB will perforate your eardrum. A decibel is one-tenth of a bel, which was named after Alexander Graham Bell, who is known for inventing the telephone.

BLAST FROM THE PAST

The Beach Boys defined the California sound of the 1960s with songs that were both joyous and thoughtful. The band's first multi-million dollar smash-hit, "Good Vibrations," was released as a single song in October 1966. With its catchy words and bouncy chorus, the sound features the usual rock lineup of guitar, bass, piano, and drums, as well as the unique additions of pipe organ and cello. The electro-theramin, a keyboard-style instrument, provides the tune's distinctive high-pitched whining sound.

The vibrations of the eardrum move three tiny bones that press on the cochlea, a spiral structure that resembles a snail's shell. Tiny hairs in the cochlea respond to sound waves. Hairs at the front of the cochlea pick up high-pitched sounds. Deeper inside, longer hairs detect those that are low-pitched. These hairs send signals to the auditory nerve, which in turn sends signals to the brain. You perceive those signals as sound.

SOUND AND NOISE

What's the difference between sound and just plain noise? Noise is unwanted sound. Like musical tastes, this can be a personal distinction. One person's song is another's racket! Typically, sound is the sensation in your ear, while noise is an unexpected or unpleasant sound. When a pesky mosquito buzzes right next to your ear, it produces an annoying noise.

What's the difference between the sounds of music and noise? Music is arranged in regular patterns of pitch and rhythm. The sounds of noise are irregular and haphazard. But people can have strong opinions about music. Have your parents ever thought your music sounded like noise to them?

ARTISTIC MIX OF NOTES, PITCH, TONE, AND RHYTHM

When you hum along to the Beach Boys' "Good Vibrations" or a tune from your personal playlist, you're responding to music. Music is a creative, artistic arrangement of sounds—a pattern of vibrations in the air and a pattern or repetition of sounds. When you sing, you send sound vibrations into the air. How can you create vibrations with musical instruments? With a bow, you can release the rich, deep sound of a cello. You can pluck a guitar or other stringed instrument. You can toot a trombone or other brass, and wail on a reed to play the sax. Try clanking a cowbell or other percussive instrument.

Notes are arrangements of musical sounds in a specific order. In a standard scale, there are eight notes—A, B, C, D, E, F, G, A. To create music, a composer arranges notes in groups, called measures or bars. Pitch is a specific frequency of sound, how high or low a sound is on a scale. Each note on the scale represents a specific pitch. Tone is the quality of these notes. Some tones are called bright or dark, while others are warm or open.

MUSICAL NOTE

With their hit song "Good Vibrations," the Beach Boys added a new phrase to the vocabulary of popular culture. People started using the term "good vibes" to mean something that evokes a good feeling or positive energy.

Rhythm patterns are the duration of and space between notes. These patterns provide the foundations of the different musical styles that you'll explore in this book.

Whether sung or played on an instrument, notes are held for a particular length of time. Music notation is a set of written symbols that specify the length and pitch of notes. We write notation from left to right in the way we jot words on paper.

Do you ever find yourself tapping your feet or bopping your head to a song? That's rhythm making you want to move. Rhythm is the pattern and emphasis of beats. Some beats may be stronger or longer or shorter or softer than others, but there's always a pattern of sounds and silences. Rhythm is the interval of measured time in a piece of music. But there's rhythm beyond music as well. In *Hearing and Writing Music: Professional Training for Today's Musician*, Ron Gorow writes, "Rhythm is everywhere: your breathing, pulse, the tides, days, seasons, life cycles, celestial motion."

FEEL THE BEAT

Until recently, researchers believed only humans could bop to different beats. But scientists recently revealed a sulphur-crested cockatoo named Snowball, who is a head-banging dancing machine! With synchronized moves, he grooves to his favorite song, "Everybody," by the Backstreet Boys.

Neurobiologist Aniruddh Patel received a viral video of Snowball bobbing, swaying, and stomping to "Everybody's" beat. Patel studies music and the brain at San Diego's Neurosciences Institute. Intrigued, he contacted Snowball's owner Irena Schultz, who lives in Indiana, and asked her to help him conduct an experiment.

His group took Snowball's favorite song and manipulated it on the computer, first slowing it down and then speeding it up. They asked Schulz to play the modified music for Snowball and videotape his reactions. The videos show that the bird will match his moves to the beat. For the slower versions, he swayed his entire body like a pendulum. But when the music got faster, he adjusted his movements to sway a little less and bob his head.

Adena Schachner, a graduate student in the psychology department of Harvard University, believes the parrot's dancing abilities may be linked to its capacity to mimic speech. Dancing may be a byproduct of vocal imitation and learning. To mimic a sound you have to listen to it and its rhythm. You have to use that information to coordinate the movement of your lips and tongue. Rock on, Snowball!

PLAYLIST

View and listen to a video of Snowball's dance. Then turn down the sound and watch it again. Can you pick up the song's beat through Snowball's moves?

WARBLING WINEGLASSES

Ben Franklin was an inventor, composer, and musician who lived from 1706 to 1790. He created the glass armonica, which was a popular musical instrument of the time made of glasses mounted on a revolving spindle, played with a moistened fingertip. Where did Franklin find the inspiration for the glass armonica? At a musical performance in London, the performer's instruments were wineglasses of different sizes filled with water. With a wet fingertip, the musician circled the glasses' rims. The glasses responded to the friction in a variety of pitches, and the resulting vibrations produced ethereal, haunting sounds.

Work with your classmates, friends, or family members to create warbling wineglasses. Experiment with varying water levels to create different pitches.

🎵 The scientific method is the way that scientists ask questions and find answers.

Scientific Method Worksheet
Questions: What are we trying to find out? What problem are we trying to solve?
Equipment: What did we use?
Methods: What did we do?
Predictions: What do we think will happen?
Results: What happened and why?

- **Start a scientific method worksheet to organize your questions and predictions.** How will the amount of water in each glass impact pitch? How much friction will be required to produce vibrations and sounds? State your hypothesis. This is an unproven idea or prediction that tries to explain certain facts or observations.

- **Experiment by pouring different amounts of water into the different wineglasses to create an octave, or set of notes from A to A.** You can use the keyboard to establish the appropriate pitch for each note. Gently tap each glass with the spoon to test for a matching pitch. Is it easy to determine if the sounds are the same? How carefully do you need to listen? Does it help to have several people listen at the same time? How can you adjust the pitch in each glass so it matches?

- **Practice playing tunes on the glasses.** Start with something simple, such as "Happy Birthday." Don't get frustrated if it doesn't work right away. Make sure your finger is wet enough. Then, mix it up! Play more complicated but familiar pieces. See if others can identify them.

- **Work together to write a fantastical poem or story, and compose a musical piece that reflects the literary work's mood.** Ben Franklin penned a dramatic literary work to be performed with an accompanist on the glass armonica. Perform the work as someone accompanies you on the warbling wineglasses.

- **How accurate were your predictions?** How would you adjust your hypothesis? How did the musical accompaniment engage emotions or activate moods during the literary piece? Why do you think the glasses produce such otherworldly sounds?

Ideas for Supplies ▼

- science journal and pencil
- stemmed wineglasses of different sizes
- water
- metal spoon
- keyboard

To investigate more, search for an online performance of a street musician playing wineglasses. You might be lucky enough to watch one in person! What do you notice about their playing technique? Explore musician William Zeitler's glass armonica pieces with a family member or friend. What emotional responses do they ignite? Listen to Mozart's "Adagio and Rondo." These are delicate pieces he composed for the glass armonica. How do the pieces suit the instrument?

SPLISH, SPLASH

Vibrations that travel through air produce sound. These vibrations cause air molecules to move. They enter the ear, where we hear through air conductivity. Can sound pass through another medium? How will water impact the way sounds travel?

With a partner or group, first explore the way sounds travel through air, and then how sounds move in the water of a bathtub or swimming pool.

- **Start a scientific method worksheet to organize your questions and predictions.** How loud and intense will sounds be when they travel through air? Will the medium of water muffle or amplify sounds? Will it be easier to hear sounds in air or water? Discuss your ideas, and brainstorm additional questions. State a hypothesis.

MUSICAL NOTE

Sound travels more than four times faster in water than in air. Air conductivity and vibrations from our eardrum allow us to hear above water. When we're submerged under water, bones in our skull vibrate to hear. Bone conductivity is 40 percent less effective than air conductivity. Does this make it easier or harder to hear underwater?

- **In the air and in turn, smack together three sets of objects, such as those suggested.** Listen to their sounds. How loud and how intense are the sounds? Then, experiment in the bathtub or in a pool. Plug one ear and keep it above water. Submerge the other ear. Repeat the process, clacking each set of objects. Judge their loudness and intensity, and record your observations.

- **Assess your findings and draw conclusions.** Were your predicted results accurate? Does water muffle or amplify sounds? To analyze your data, try using computer software to generate a graph that illustrates the results of your experiment.

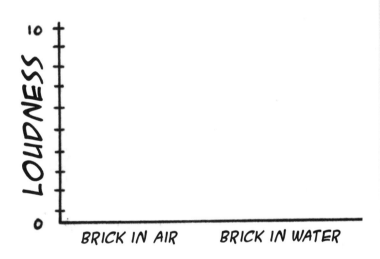

To investigate more, gather additional objects to test, or change the experiment's conditions. For example, what would happen if you plugged both ears during the water tests?

BLAST FROM THE PAST

With its wailing sax, honky-tonk piano, and joyful humor, "Splish Splash" was a 1958 breakout hit for Bobby Darin (1936–1973). Challenged to write a song that contained the line, "Splish, splash, I was takin' a bath," Darin dashed off the smash single. He claimed he composed the hit in 12 minutes! "Splish Splash" sold over a million copies and launched Darin's career as a rock and roll idol.

LISTEN UP! AUDITORY ACUITY

Auditory acuity is the keenness or sharpness of hearing. Acuity can vary with each of your ears, and it varies from person to person. Work with your teacher, a classmate, or a parent to investigate individual auditory acuity. Experiment with a subject's hearing as he or she covers each ear in turn and listens to sounds from a variety of distances and angles.

- **Start a scientific method worksheet and data chart to organize your questions, predictions, and data.** Share theories about how acuity will be impacted with distance and under different conditions. Discuss your ideas, and brainstorm questions. State a hypothesis.

- **With masking tape, make an X for the subject to stand on.** Mark a line on the floor 5 feet away (1½ meters) from the X and more lines every 5 feet. Note the distance on each piece of tape as you position it on the floor.

- **Ask the subject to stand on the X, and close his or her eyes tightly.** Have your subject cup a hand over each ear in turn. Ring a bell or chime from each distance marked. Can your subject identify where you are standing?

- **Experiment with producing sounds at different angles.** For example, raise your hands above your head to ring the bell, or lower them below your knees. How do these angles impact your subject's ability to identify the distance of the sound? Note all of your observations on the data chart.

- science journal and pencil
- masking tape
- tape measure
- marker
- bell or chime

Distance in Feet (Meters)	Sound's Angle	Right Ear Covered	Left Ear Covered
5 (1.5)			
10 (3)			
15 (4.5)			
20 (6.1)			
25 (7.6)			

To investigate more, switch places and have your subject test you to compare results. How can you create a spreadsheet or graph to present your findings? Analyze your results and assess your hypothesis.

PUMP UP THE VOLUME

Sound is a form of energy that travels in vibrations. The loudness of sound is measured in units called decibels, which is the force of sound waves against the ear. As sound grows louder, decibels increase. Work with others to experiment with different decibel levels. Experiment with decibels by creating a mini sound trampoline. Can we hear and see the sound?

- **Start a scientific method worksheet to organize your questions and predictions.** Do you think the vibrations of sound can physically move objects? How loud would it have to be? State your hypothesis.

- **Cover a bowl with plastic wrap to make a mini sound trampoline.** Place small pieces of dried pasta on top and set the trampoline on a speaker. What do you think will happen to the pasta when you play music?

- **Place the sound trampoline on top of a speaker.** Test different types of music, such as tunes with driving beats and pounding drums and those that are gentler. How does the pasta respond as you turn up the volume and increase decibel levels? Complete the data chart as you conduct your tests.

- **Work in groups to videotape the sound trampoline each time you test it.** Share your videotapes and compare the results. How do different pieces of music impact the pasta? With what piece of music do you observe the most noticeable responses?

Ideas for Supplies ▼

- science journal and pencil
- wide-mouthed bowl
- plastic wrap
- small dried pasta
- speaker
- variety of music
- data chart
- video recorder

Piece of Music	Volume Setting	Response of Object

To investigate more, test a variety of music genres. Make a new chart to track at what volume levels you prefer different songs. Do you notice that you prefer certain genres softer or louder than others? What about your favorite songs? Do you turn the volume up for songs you like better and down for songs you don't like as much?

Chapter 2 ▶
Colonial Times and the Music of Slave Life

How much did the slave trade influence American music?

🎵 Music gives us a chance to peek into the past to learn what people's lives were like, what they valued, and how they entertained themselves.

How have America's diverse music genres evolved? To understand American music, you have to go back to the very beginning, when the country was forming. Many of America's sounds have been influenced by the people held in slavery, whose roots were in Africa, and by the colonists who came from Europe.

Did you know that spirituals and folk songs inspired country music? Spirituals are religious songs—folk hymns based on stories in the Bible that were sung by slaves. Jazz, which originated in New Orleans, also evolved from slave music. Blues began with African-American traditions in the South, hopped the rails north, and became electrified in Chicago, where it maintains a strong identity. R&B, which combines jazz and blues, was rock's precursor. Even hip-hop's urban sounds trace their roots to Africa.

Colonial America was the time between 1607 and 1776, when people from Europe settled in colonies along the East Coast of what is now the United States of America. Let's see how America's diverse sound roots sprouted and took hold in colonial times, influenced by slavery, religion, and European tradition.

AMERICA'S FIRST SONGBOOK

When the group of colonists we now call Puritans left England to practice their religion freely, an ocean separated them from their homeland. But their songs came with them.

Twenty years after the Puritans and the rest of the Pilgrims first arrived in North America, the Massachusetts Bay Colony's first printer issued *The Whole Booke of Psalmes Faithfully Translated into English Metre* in 1640. Better known as *The Bay Psalm Book*, this was the first book ever printed in the New World. It was a pocket-sized translation of the Bible's Book of Psalms from Hebrew. *The Bay Psalm Book* was based on an earlier edition that colonists brought with them from England.

According to the Library of Congress, *The Bay Psalm Book* "represents what was most sacred to the Puritans—a faithful translation of God's Word, to be sung in worship by the entire congregation." This little songbook reflects the important values of political freedom and religious liberty on which the United States of America was founded.

🎵 The United States Library of Congress is the world's largest library, containing more than 144 million items. Among its treasure trove of rare books is one of 11 surviving copies of *The Bay Psalm Book*, now a piece of musical and political history.

Notable Quotable

"Music is an art of sounding, not writing."

—Richard Crawford, who wrote *America's Musical Life: A History*

Folk songs are ordinary songs made up by ordinary people—regular folks. As the song changes over time, it becomes the creation of many people.

MUSICAL NOTE

Beginning in the early 1900s, folklorists traveled the country recording the musical styles of various communities. In 1952, the "Anthology of American Folk Music" exposed people all over the country to this music. By the late 1950s, folk music was popular on college campuses and America enjoyed a folk revival, focused on civil rights and free speech issues of the day.

ORAL TRADITION: FOLK MUSIC

What's the first thing you learned to sing? Maybe your parents sang the alphabet to you over and over again, or "Twinkle, Twinkle Little Star," and soon you were singing along. You were far too young to be reading the words. Long before MP3 devices, before CDs and albums, stereos and gramophones, even before the printing press and written language, people relied on a critical human technology—memory.

The New World's earliest European immigrants journeyed from the Netherlands, England, Scotland, and Ireland. They traveled with songs packed in the trunks of their hearts and minds. Immigrants spread emotional folk songs and ballads throughout Colonial America, which had been passed down from as early as the 1200s. Sharing by heart, people added special flourishes to make renditions distinctly their own. Stories and songs changed and evolved as they were told and retold, and sprinkled with inside jokes and personal commentary.

A folk song is any type of music that tells the story of what life was like in a certain time and culture. Traditional folk music came from farm and factory workers of the lower classes of the Old World. The original author is usually unknown and the songs are passed down orally and changed through families and other social groups.

The ballad is an important part of folk music. A ballad is a narrative verse set to song. It tells a poetic and melodramatic story, real or imagined, through short stanzas.

Many ballads tell tragic tales of murder or accidental death, and contain supernatural elements. Although ballads are packed with emotional power, their performers sing them with a calm voice to let the vivid words speak for themselves.

The tragic English love ballad "Barbara Allen" was first introduced in North America around 1666. Who first created the song? Centuries and generations later, it remains a mystery. The mournful song changed as artists tweaked details, invented character names, and made it their own. Some named characters after their own lost loves or set the tale in their own villages. Today there are at least 92 variations of "Barbara Allen."

HUMAN CARGO

The transatlantic slave trade formed the world's largest forced migration. From about 1500 to 1800, more than 10 million men, women, and children from West and Central Africa were enslaved. Through the slave trade, dealers transported people as human cargo to the Americas and sold them in the New World. Slaves labored in the fields of coffee, cotton, and tobacco plantations or worked inside homes.

Economic development in the New World depended on slave labor. Slaves formed the workforce. Many were experts at raising crops in tropical climates and at keeping cattle. Their agricultural know-how and hard work in the fields and in mines made their owners wealthy. Since slaves were considered property, they got nothing in return. They earned no wages, owned no land, and had no rights.

PLAYLIST

Explore a variety of renditions of "Barbara Allen." You might listen to British punk-folk singer Frank Turner, German alto Andreas Scholl, and American folk singers Joan Baez and Pete Seeger. Notice variations in style, vocals, and tempo. How do the lyrics differ? Analyze the unique spin each artist gives the ballad.

Notable Quotable

"**Slaves sing most when they are most unhappy. The songs of the slave represent the sorrows of his heart; and he is relieved by them, only as an aching heart is relieved by its tears.**"

—Frederick Douglass, (1818–1895), an abolitionist who escaped from slavery and devoted his life to equality

SOUNDS OF SLAVERY

Because of Africa's enormous size, its people, and traditions are, and always have been, varied. Captured and taken from their homes all over Africa, the people forced to work as slaves in the Americas spoke many different languages. To communicate, they used a universal language—music.

Though cut off from their homelands, slaves kept their rich cultural identities and oral traditions alive. In Africa, music was the heartbeat of life. It expressed the feelings of entire communities. Slaves transported this importance of music to the New World. They sang frequently, expressing themselves by joining in sound and movement.

Forced to toil at backbreaking labor, slaves raised their voices in work songs and field hollers. Music relieved some of the drudgery of their repetitive work.

Many songs involved a call-and-response pattern with a caller, or leader, singing across a field of crops. A group sang out a chorus in response. With on-the-spot creativity, singers added unique touches. They embellished songs with quirky harmonies and tones. They synchronized the rhythm of their songs with their work, such as swinging axes, plucking cotton, and hoeing tobacco fields.

MUSICAL NOTE

To enhance their voices, during their free time slaves made use of homemade instruments like banjos, tambourines, calabashes, washboards, pots and pans, and spoons.

To replicate African instruments, slaves devised inventive uses for household items. Cider jugs became wind instruments. Spoons kept a percussive beat. From the dried and hollowed shells of calabashes, they crafted lute-like stringed instruments and percussive shakers.

African singing was totally new to European ears. The sound was much more nasal, loud, and shrill than what settlers were used to. The falsetto, shouts, groans, and deep rumblings were all sounds that were unique to African cultures. The bells, flutes, horns, marimbas, gourd shakers, and drums that ranged in size and sound were exotic instruments at the time. And the spontaneous and improvisational performance style of the slaves impressed Europeans.

SPIRITUALS

In spirituals, European hymns met with the African oral tradition to create a new American genre. As described by Soprano Randye Jones, "Spirituals are songs created by the Africans who were captured and brought to the United States to be sold into slavery. This stolen race was deprived of their languages, families, and culture; yet, their masters could not take away their music."

In the early years of the slave trade, African religious beliefs were extremely diverse. But music and dance were almost always features of their religious practices. Some colonists promised slaves freedom in exchange for converting to Christianity. Desperate for freedom, many slaves adopted the Christian religion of their masters, particularly the Baptist faith.

MUSICAL NOTE

The mournful spiritual "Go Down, Moses" illustrates a personal interpretation of the Old Testament's Book of Exodus 8:1. "And the Lord spoke unto Moses, Go unto Pharaoh, and say unto him, Thus saith the Lord, Let my people go, that they may serve me." The refrain, "let my people go," addressed the rebellion of Moses. He freed the Israelites from slavery and led them out of Egypt. But the spiritual also draws a parallel between the Exodus story and slavery. It expresses the struggle for freedom of enslaved Africans.

🎵 **"Follow the Drinking Gourd" is written in a minor key to evoke mysterious feelings.**

Even as they adopted Christian beliefs, enslaved Africans kept some of their own musical expressions alive. By about 1700, slaves were expressing their faith through song and traditional rhythms. Pounding broomsticks and stomping feet provided percussion. Chants and call-and-response lyrics were links to African forms. Even slaves denied the privilege of reading and writing could listen to, memorize, and retell Bible stories through powerful spirituals.

Spirituals were sacred folk songs shared in worship services. They contained complex layers of meaning. On the surface, spirituals retold Bible stories. Underneath though, they held deeper messages. They shared the sorrows and degradation of slave life and their inspirational lyrics urged hope and tolerance.

FOLLOW THE DRINKING GOURD

To express deep, hidden feelings of anger, fear, and a thirst for freedom, slaves relied on coded messages in the musical language of spirituals and folk songs. Some people believe "Follow the Drinking Gourd" contained secret messages hidden in its words.

These messages urged slaves to follow the Big Dipper north along the Underground Railroad. The metaphorical railroad was a secret network of safe houses. Abolitionists there assisted slaves escaping to freedom in the North.

How could a person fleeing at night find north? The fixed North Star in the night sky showed the way. It never changes position and always points north. Slaves were familiar with the Big Dipper and knew that two of its stars always pointed to the North Star. So by finding the Big Dipper, which resembles a giant, hollowed-out gourd, they could locate the pointer stars and head north.

In 1849, Harriet Tubman may have followed the drinking gourd to escape slavery in Maryland and flee to safety in Pennsylvania. She was the most famous conductor on the Underground Railroad, leading 70 slaves to freedom.

PLAYLIST

"Follow the Drinking Gourd" has been recorded over 200 times and remains a cherished song of resistance and hope. Listen to the first commercially released version of the song, recorded by The Weavers in 1951.

Compare it to a bluegrass version recorded by the Homestead Pickers in 2003 and Taj Mahal's folk version from 1991.

I SEE THE NORTH STAR. THIS WAY!

PATTIN' JUBA

After an uprising in 1739, the Negro Act of 1740 was a law passed in South Carolina to legally control the actions of slaves. They were not allowed to assemble in groups, raise food, earn money, or learn to read English. At the same time, some plantation owners banned slaves from beating drums. Owners feared slaves would use drumbeats to send secret codes over long distances and arrange uprisings.

But the ban couldn't stop the music. Slaves resisted and rebelled with creativity. Through juba dance, or "pattin' juba," they used their bodies as instruments. Briskly clapping their hands, slapping their legs and thighs, and tapping the ground with their feet, juba dancers created percussive sounds.

Irish and Scottish indentured laborers who stomped to lively fiddling influenced juba. Slaves may have imitated Irish jigs and step dances and Scottish clog dances. Over time, juba morphed into tap, a brisk, rhythmic, uniquely American form of step dance. All of these percussive forms influenced the "buck and wing" dance style, which is a lively solo tap dance with sharp foot accents, leg flings, and heel clicks.

William Henry Lane (1825–1852) popularized juba. Born free in Rhode Island, Lane combined patting juba with dances he learned from his Irish neighbor to create a new dance form. Using the stage name Master Juba, Lane played the tambourine and banjo and danced his way into huge popularity, performing in dance competitions all over the United States and for royalty in Europe. Lane is considered the inventor of tap dancing.

BEAT OF THE DRUM

In the United States, slaves maintained their African musical traditions and techniques while creatively adopting European styles and instruments. To keep time, many used juba and djembe drums, which they played with their hands instead of sticks. Traditional goblet djembe drums are constructed of wooden or clay bases with a drumhead of goat or other animal skin stretched across the top. A drumhead produces vibrations.

Work with your classmates or a group to construct drums from common household items, such as clay pots, deep metal bowls, and wide-brimmed plastic storage containers. Then investigate the types of sounds these different drums produce.

- **Start with some ideas and theories.** How will the size and shape of a hollow container impact sound? How does striking the drum in different places change vibrations and sound? How are powerful, resonant sounds produced? Discuss other questions with your group and formulate a hypothesis.

- **Make your drums and analyze their sounds.** Create a table to record the type of drum you are testing, what you strike it with, where you strike it, and the type of sound it makes. What happens when you strike different parts of the drumhead? Can you think of other ideas for drums now that you understand them better?

To investigate more, make more drums using your new knowledge. Play your drums to improvise along to some of your favorite tunes. If you make an MP3 recording you can share your drumming with others.

Ideas for Supplies ▼

- journal and pencil
- hollow containers such as clay pots and metal bowls
- drumhead materials such as plastic shrink-wrap insulating film, cloth, and cowhide
- string and rubberbands for insulating film
- scissors
- blow dryer
- objects to strike the drum
- audio recorder

MUSICAL NOTE

Through music, Native American cultures share oral narratives and histories. Drumming and percussive instruments, including rattles and bells, are important features of their musical traditions.

BECOME A BALLADEER

With the human technology of memory, balladeers learned stories, sprinkled on their own spicy flavorings, and spread ballads through oral tradition.

A ballad's rhyme scheme can vary. If it is a-b-a-b, the first and third lines and second and fourth lines rhyme, as in the first stanza of "Barbara Allen":

> *'Twas in the merry month of May (a)*
> *When green buds were a-swellin', (b)*
> *Sweet William on his deathbed lay (a)*
> *For the love of Barbara Allen. (b)*

If the rhyme scheme is a-b-c-b, the second and fourth lines rhyme, as in the second stanza of "Barbara Allen":

> *Slowly, slowly she got up, (a)*
> *And slowly she went nigh him, (b)*
> *And all she said when she got there, (c)*
> *"Young man, I think you're dyin.'" (b)*

Swellin' and Allen *and* nigh him *and* dyin' *are near rhymes—they don't exactly rhyme as* May *and* lay *do. The phrase* merry month of May *employs alliteration, which is repetition of like sounds at the beginnings of words.*

- **With your classmates or friends, write and perform a four-verse ballad.** Ballads aren't always set to music, but they always tell a story.

- **Choose an incident from one of your favorite books to dramatize.** Select a scene that's thrilling and emotional, one that places the main character in a dangerous or difficult situation. Brainstorm ideas, and jot down notes.

PLAYLIST

Today, slow, romantic pop tunes, including Beyoncé's "Listen," Adele's "Someone Like You," Taylor Swift's "All Too Well," and Rihanna's "Diamonds" are called ballads.

- **Create a list of questions to consider. Decide on your rhyme scheme.** Will you use only exact rhymes or include near rhymes? Do you want to consider a refrain at the end of each verse? Will you set it to a familiar song, or recite it as a poem? Do you want to use musical instruments?

- **Rehearse your completed work and perform the ballad for others.** Ask your audience to share their responses. Challenge an audience member to recite part of the ballad. Did he or she recite it from memory or make changes?

> To investigate more, write another ballad with a different rhyme scheme. Change as many variables as you can think of. Record both your ballads and observe the differences.

Resonance is the sound a vibrating object produces.

LIFT EVERY VOICE AND SING

How do we sing? The vocal cords are made up of two membranes stretched across the larynx. When air passes through the vocal cords, they vibrate. Sound resonates in the sinus cavities, throat, and chest, which are called resonators. The lips, tongue, teeth, and palate, known as articulators, work together to make the sound leave your body.

Investigate the vibrations of your resonators as you sing along with a recorded song or croon on your own.

- **Sing out loud! As you do, press your fingers gently against your throat and then against your sinuses.** Rest your palm lightly on your chest. Create a written list of questions to consider. Some ideas are:

  a. What do you feel?

  b. Can you feel vibrations anywhere else?

  c. Where are the vibrations strongest?

  d. Why do you think a particular resonator produces its specific vibrations?

PLAYLIST

The spiritual "Lift Every Voice and Sing" is often called the African American national anthem. James W. Johnson wrote the inspirational poem in 1899. His brother John R. Johnson set it to music. View or listen to soul singer Ray Charles' gospel rendition and Wintley Phipps' booming baritone interpretation. Pay attention to how the different styles make you feel.

- **Experiment with singing at different pitches, volumes, note lengths, and head positions.** Assess the different sounds you produce. Record your observations on the chart and analyze your findings.

Resonator	Pitch: Low vs. High	Volume: Soft vs. Loud	Length: Brief vs. Prolonged	Head Position: Straight vs. Tilted
throat				
sinuses				
chest				

To investigate more, try humming instead of singing, or explore the way your articulators respond to vibrations. Experiment with different types of songs, such as soft rock and loud, syncopated rap. How do they impact your results?

Lift Every Voice and Sing

Lift every voice and sing, till earth and Heaven ring,

Ring with the harmonies of liberty;

Let our rejoicing rise, high as the listening skies,

Let it resound loud as the rolling sea.

Sing a song full of the faith that the dark past has taught us,

Sing a song full of the hope that the present has brought us;

Facing the rising sun of our new day begun,

Let us march on till victory is won.

A MAP TO FREEDOM

There were many escape routes out of the South, but the route detailed in "Follow the Drinking Gourd" is a famous one.

The song used code to tell slaves to follow the Tombigbee River, which runs through Mississippi and Alabama, to the Tennessee River. The Tennessee River runs through Alabama, Tennessee, and Kentucky. There, it flows into the Ohio River, a common escape route into the free state of Illinois.

- **Look at the explanation of the lyrics and refer to a United States map to follow the path.** Can you follow the trail?

- **Map out another route on the map. Write your own verses with coded geographical messages. Include a code-cracker to explain the messages.** Brainstorm creative, poetic ways to assign a second level of meaning to your lyrics.

MUSICAL NOTE

Have you ever told stories around a campfire? What made your story stand out? As stories and songs flow from one person to another through the oral tradition, original pieces change. People add in jokes and dramatic touches. A story with a grain of truth can evolve into one that's completely imaginative.

Lyrics	Coded Meaning
When the sun comes back,	Leave in spring when the days are getting longer.
and the first quail calls, follow the drinking gourd	Quail in Alabama start calling to each other in early to mid-April. Then find the Big Dipper and the North Star and head north.
The old man is a-waiting for to carry you to freedom if you follow the drinking gourd	"Ole man" is a sailing term for "Captain." This is said to refer to Peg Leg Joe who was once a sailor. Peg Leg Joe led many slaves to freedom.
The riverbank will make a very good road	Follow along the Tombigbee River out of Alabama.
The dead trees will show you the way Left foot, peg foot, traveling on, Follow the drinking gourd	According to H.B. Parks, Peg Leg Joe marked trees and other landmarks "with charcoal or mud in the outline of a human left foot and a round spot in place of the right foot."
The river ends between two hills, Follow the drinking gourd	The source of the Tombigbee River is near Woodall Mountain, the high point in Mississippi. There is a neighboring hill, but Woodall itself looks like two gentle hills.
There's another river on the other side, Follow the drinking gourd	The Tennessee River is on the other side. Following it north leads to the Ohio River border with Illinois.
Where the great big river meets the little river Follow the drinking gourd The old man is awaiting for to carry you to freedom If you follow the drinking gourd.	The Tennessee meets the "great" Ohio River in Paduchah, Kentucky. There you'll find Peg Leg Joe who will take you across to the free state of Illinois.

Ideas for Supplies

- **journal and pencil**
- **map of the United States**
- **colored pencils**

To investigate more, use coded lyrics to create a route near your house or school. See if your friends or family can follow it! How will they know if they're on the right track? How do they know when they've arrived?

Chapter 3 ▶
The Birth of a New Nation: Patriotic Music

How did war influence
American music?

THERE WE SEE THE MEN AND THE BOYS,

AS THICK AS HASTY PUDDING!

♪ Patriotic songs like "Yankee Doodle" and "The Star-Spangled Banner" expressed common pride and hope for the future. They were also played for entertainment and to ease the burden on troops as they marched. Now these songs are part of our national heritage.

When the colonists declared their independence from England in 1776, the colonial period of American history ended. In the years leading up to the Revolutionary War, why did settlers in the colonies become so angry at the British government? Because the British made more and more laws to control the colonists and raise their taxes.

The colonists had no representation in their government. This means they could not vote for the people who governed them. The colonists had no way to influence their taxes or the decisions being made for them from across the ocean.

With the Tea Act of 1773, the government gave the British East India Company a monopoly on selling tea in the colonies. The colonists rebelled and a mob boarded three ships in Boston Harbor carrying East India Company tea. The mob dumped 342 crates of tea in the harbor in an incident that came to be known as the Boston Tea Party. More acts of rebellion followed and the colonists eventually went to war in a fight for independence.

"YANKEE DOODLE," 1760s

Do you know the words and the tune to "Yankee Doodle?" Like many kids growing up in America, you probably do. Kids all over the country sing, "I'm a Yankee Doodle dandy . . ." But what do these words really mean?

Like a lot of folk songs, "Yankee Doodle's" origins aren't totally clear. According to music tradition, a British army surgeon during the French and Indian War wrote the song to amuse a patient. He was making fun of the poorly trained and ill-equipped American colonists who fought with the British against the French over territory in Ohio and Canada.

Yankee was an insulting word for America's colonists. In the language of the day, *doodle* meant a foolish person and a *dandy* was used to describe a man overly focused on fancy clothes and hairstyles.

On the morning of April 19, 1775, British soldiers marched into battle in Lexington, Massachusetts, on the first day of the Revolutionary War. They sang the catchy tune and marched to its rhythm, teasing the colonial forces who they still viewed as unsophisticated and sloppy.

In June 1775, after the inexperienced colonial troops caused the British significant casualties in the Battle of Bunker Hill, the rebels took control of the cheerful song and turned it around. They wrote countless new verses that cleverly ridiculed the British. New lyrics praised their commander George Washington and encouraged pride and unity. The Americans were proud to be called Yankees, and "Yankee Doodle" became a patriotic song. Led by a corps of fife and drums, troops marched rhythmically along to their new rallying cry.

The harsh spirit of the Revolutionary War era produced "Yankee Doodle," which has become an American classic. Its beat made it a great marching song.

PLAYLIST

This is the first stanza and chorus of the original version of "Yankee Doodle." You can download a printable version of the full lyrics and the musical score from the Library of Congress.

Yankee Doodle

Father and I went down to camp,

Along with Captain Gooding,

There we see the men and boys,

As thick as hasty pudding.

Chorus

Yankee doodle keep it up,

Yankee doodle, dandy,

Mind the music and the step,

And with the girls be handy.

MUSICAL NOTE

British and colonial armies used fife and drum music to direct the movement of their soldiers. A company of about 100 men had one or two fifers and drummers. When eight or ten companies formed a regiment, the musicians formed a regimental band. The band used musical signals to position the troops onto and off of the battlefield and to change their formations, as well as to halt, march, or change their direction.

"THE STAR-SPANGLED BANNER," 1814

Peace did not last for long after the Revolutionary War ended and America gained its independence from Great Britain. America was a new country with new challenges and new allies. France had supported America during its war of independence, and many Americans felt that their new country should support France in its long war with Great Britain. As Britain continued to interfere in American's affairs, America finally declared war on the British Empire in 1812, beginning nearly three years of brutal battles.

Britain was determined to crush the rebellious Americans with an attack on Washington, DC, America's new capital. In August 1814, about 4,000 British troops set fire to the White House, the Library of Congress, the Capitol building, and other public buildings.

With the nation's capital in rubble, the British planned a double attack by land and water on Baltimore, Maryland, then the third-largest city in America. But after 24 hours of heavy attack, American forces defending Baltimore still held onto their city.

Lawyer and poet Francis Scott Key (1780–1843) was a prisoner on a British ship 8 miles away (13 kilometers). When he saw the American flag still flying the next day, he knew the Americans had not surrendered and Baltimore was saved. Deeply moved, Keys scrawled a poem on the back of a letter jammed in his pocket, which he called "The Defense of Fort McHenry."

A year later, Key set the poem to the tune of a popular British song. When the song was performed in public, the singer called the song, "The Star-Spangled Banner," and the title stuck. The honored song of loyalty and praise is an important symbol of an American identity and it officially became the national anthem through an act of Congress in 1931.

🎵 **"The Star-Spangled Banner" is now played at events all over the country. You'll hear it before kids' sports games and Olympic competitions, on U.S. military bases at the beginning and end of each day, and at local festivals and community gatherings, especially on the Fourth of July.**

OH! SAY DOES THAT STAR-SPANGLED BANNER YET WAVE...

"BATTLE HYMN OF THE REPUBLIC," 1862

In September 2001, following the 9/11 terrorist attacks on the World Trade Center, the United States held a service of remembrance and prayer in the National Cathedral in Washington, DC. Then-president George W. Bush and former presidents Jimmy Carter, Bill Clinton, and Gerald Ford mingled their voices with the congregation as everyone sang "Battle Hymn of the Republic."

During the 1800s, both the American flag and "The Star-Spangled Banner" were widespread symbols of patriotism. But the country was increasingly divided over the issue of slavery. As the United States expanded west of the original 13 colonies, there was constant disagreement over the spread of slavery to those areas.

Neither the North, whose people did not allow slavery, nor the South, whose people relied on slavery, wanted the balance shifted in the other side's favor. If more states forbade slavery than allowed it, the country might vote to end it everywhere. The South feared that their plantation economy of cotton and tobacco would collapse without the large, cheap labor force that slavery provided. The Civil War began in 1861 after South Carolina seceded from the Union. Several other southern states joined South Carolina to form the Confederate States of America.

During the Civil War, the song "John Brown's Body" became a popular marching song among Union troops from the North. Set to the tune of a popular church song ("Say, Brothers, Will You Meet Us?"), the song's lyrics tell the tragic tale of abolitionist John Brown. After leading 21 men on a raid to seize a government stash of weapons at Harper's Ferry, West Virginia, in 1859, Brown was put to death by hanging. He had planned to give the weapons to slaves to start a war in Virginia against slavery.

John Brown's body lies a-mouldering in the grave,

John Brown's body lies a-mouldering in the grave,

John Brown's body lies a-mouldering in the grave,

His soul is marching on!

How did this song become "Battle Hymn of the Republic?" In 1861, President Lincoln invited Julia Ward Howe, a poet and dedicated abolitionist, to visit Washington, DC. On a tour of Union army camps in neighboring Virginia, her carriage inched along roads clogged with marching soldiers singing "John Brown's Body." Civilians joined in, cheering the troops. Moved by the day's events, Howe was determined to write a poem more suited to the rousing music.

In 1862, *Atlantic Monthly* magazine published her poem, titled "Battle Hymn of the Republic." It became the anthem of the Union cause and remains one of the most cherished pieces of art produced during the Civil War. Its importance to America's identity and the fight against slavery remains today.

MINSTREL SHOWS AND VAUDEVILLE

Starting in the early 1840s and continuing through the Civil War era, popular entertainment reflected racist attitudes still prevailing in America. Minstrel shows featured white entertainers dressed as plantation slaves. They darkened their faces using burnt cork and imitated black musical and dance forms. Some of America's most famous songs, including "Oh Susanna" and "Camptown Races" came from minstrel shows.

After the Civil War, American society began to change. With a major move from rural to urban areas came a growing number of white-collar workers. This expanding middle class with steady earning power enjoyed more money and more free time to spend it. Vaudeville leapt onto the stage as a spectacular way to do both and it reigned as the most popular form of family entertainment through the early 1900s. Shows were part-theater, part-circus, and part-joke-o-rama.

PLAYLIST

View and listen to Julia Ward Howe's complete lyrics of the "Battle Hymn of the Republic." The first stanza and the chorus are what people hear most often. Why do you think the tune has lasted and been so popular for over 150 years?

MUSICAL NOTE

Minstrel shows frequently included the same stereotypical characters. These included Jim Crow as a carefree slave, Mr. Tambo as a joyous musician, and Zip Coon as a free black man attempting to be from an upper class. Minstrel shows portrayed black people as lazy, simple, not very smart, and happy to be slaves.

Vaudeville offered a variety of short stage acts that ranged from mesmerizing Shakespearean actors to heart-stopping daredevil acrobats. Singers, dancers, jugglers, comedians, and animal acts promised something for everyone. People flocked to the shows. Whether they luxuriated in velvet cushions at vaudeville palaces, or squished together on wooden riverboat seats, audiences went crazy for the shared experience.

At home during this time, families gathered around the piano to sing popular songs such as "Daisy Bell" and "In the Good Old Summertime." As advances in printing made it cheaper to print sheet music, publishers issued vast amounts of parlor music, often with elaborate covers that illustrated popular culture. Sheet music became a perfect place for American companies to advertise their products. The margins of sheet music were even used during World War I to promote the war effort. "Food will win the war. Don't waste it!" appeared on sheet music published by Jos. W. Stern.

WORLD WAR I, 1914–1918

For much of World War I, America stayed on the sidelines while France, Russia, and Great Britain fought against Germany. But on April 6, 1917, the United States finally declared war against Germany and entered the conflict. World War I was largely a series of land battles fought from trenches. But advances in technology turned the battle into what is considered the first "modern" war. The catastrophic might of chemical weapons, massive tanks, and machine guns killed millions worldwide.

Some music of the era expressed unity and patriotism. On the day the United States entered World War I, George M. Cohan composed "Over There," which became one of the most famous songs of the war. On his way to work, Cohan couldn't help but notice newspaper headlines bursting with the announcement of America's involvement in the war. With a spark of inspiration, he created the rallying chorus,

O-ver there, o-ver there

Send the word, send the word, o-ver there

That the Yanks are com-ing, the Yanks are com-ing

The drums rum-tum-ming ev'-ry where.

By the time Cohan arrived at work, he had the verses, the chorus, the tune, and the title. The song sold more than two million copies before the end of the war and earned Cohan a Congressional Gold Medal.

But not everyone supported the war effort and there were many artists and performers who expressed this sentiment. In fact, the first big hit of the war, Alfred Bryan's and Al Piantadosi's "I Didn't Raise My Boy to Be a Soldier," spoke of widespread American skepticism about joining the war. Its mournful chorus sang of a mother's sorrow:

I didn't raise my boy to be a soldier

I brought him up to be my pride and joy.

The song humanized the enemy "over there" with the following lyrics,

Who dares to put a musket on his shoulder

To shoot some other mother's darling boy?

BLAST FROM THE PAST

In 1913, with World War I looming, George Gershwin (1898–1937) landed his first job in the music industry. He was only 15 years old! It was the start of a brilliant career that eventually made him one of the most sought-after musical composers in America. In an era before new recordings were widely available and sheet music was downloadable, music stores employed songpluggers to perform and promote sheet music. Pluggers like Gershwin sat playing new music at a piano positioned in an in-store balcony, giving shoppers a chance to sample the sounds before making a purchase. How does this compare to the way you can sample music before you buy it?

"GIMME FIFE!"

The fife is a wind instrument related to the flute and recorder. A wind instrument is a resonator—the tube—where a column of air vibrates when the player blows into or over the mouthpiece. The length of the tube and the way the vibrating column of air is changed determine the pitch of the sound. In medieval Europe the fife was used to play folk music for dancing.

The Revolutionary War period featured the fife played in the key of B flat or C. At the time, fifes were made from wood such as maple, walnut, cherry, cocuswood, and boxwood. Explore the sounds you can produce with a homemade flute, experimenting with posture, breathing, mouth positions, and finger positions.

* **Before you begin construction, sketch a design plan.** Indicate hole placement and measurements for spacing. What materials can you use? How long do you want your flute to be? How will you make the cuts for finger holes sharply defined? You will need to cut an embouchure hole in one end. This is the hole you'll blow into.

- **Build your flute according to your design.** The finger holes should not be ragged or too large to be covered by your fingers. The end of the flute with the embouchure needs to be plugged with a stopper to complete the flute. This way air cannot escape from both ends.

- **Holding a flute and using the embouchure hole can be tricky.** Musicians hold flutes horizontally to the right. They position the left hand with fingers curved toward themselves and knuckles away. One finger hovers over each of the three finger holes. The thumb rests beneath the instrument. Flutists position the right hand with fingers curved away and knuckles inward. With the thumb resting beneath the flute, three fingers poise above the remaining holes. Practice holding your flute. Try to keep your head upright and your arms relaxed. Are you comfortable? Check out your form in the mirror!

- **To produce sounds, flutists direct their breath into the embouchure hole.** They release breath from the lungs and through the position of the lips. With a relaxed face, they control only lip muscles. To try it out, purse your lip muscles over the hole. Blow a tight, quick stream of air across the opening. How can you make the clearest sound? How can you change the sounds you make?

> To investigate more, design and construct flutes with other materials, such as bamboo or PVC pipe. How do the sounds you produce differ and compare? Can you teach yourself to play "Yankee Doodle?"

Ideas for Supplies

- journal and pencil
- ruler
- scissors
- tube for the body of the instrument
- letter opener, screwdriver, or pen
- a stopper such as a plastic cap, cork, or cardboard circle

OH, SAY, CAN YOU SING?

"The Star-Spangled Banner" is one of the most challenging songs to sing, even for highly accomplished pros! The song requires a wide vocal range. It begins at the lowest range of the voice and soars to the highest. The song's low and high notes can be tough to reach. On top of that, its complex lyrics are easy to get wrong. Give the anthem your own spin!

- **Work with your teacher, classmates, or parent to explore different renditions of the national anthem.** Use your discoveries to arrange your own piece. Brainstorm some features to observe.

- **Note your observations and share your comments as you:**

  - View singer Whitney Houston's emotional solo at the 1991 Super Bowl. Many consider Houston's the definitive performance. How does she create a powerful delivery?

  - Compare Houston's performance with Alicia Keys's R&B interpretation at the 2013 Super Bowl.

  - Watch the a cappella performance of singer-songwriter Christina Aguilera at the 2011 Super Bowl. Even the talented, multiple Grammy winner missed some of the tricky lyrics. Can you hear where Aguilera accidentally sang, "What so proudly we watched at the twilight's last gleaming," instead of, "O'er the ramparts we watched, were so gallantly streaming"?

MUSICAL NOTE

In 2000, before she became one of the world's most successful pop-country artists, Taylor Swift (1989—) sang the national anthem for 20,000 basketball fans at a Philadelphia 76ers game. She was 11 years old!

Ideas for Supplies ▼

- journal and pencil
- computer
- keyboard or musical instruments

- View Beyoncé's lip-synched rendition at President Obama's 2013 inaugural ceremony. Most people praised the moving performance but some critics felt the singer shouldn't have relied on a pre-recorded piece. The recording did guarantee a flawless performance during a solemn occasion in front of a global audience. What are the positive and negative points of lip-synching?

- Check out the dramatic, electric-guitar instrumental of Jimi Hendrix at Woodstock in 1969. How does it compare to vocal versions? How does drumming add impact?

To investigate more, think about which rendition most resonated with you and why. Which features influenced your opinions? Share your ideas. Then use those musical influences to arrange your own musical or instrumental performance of the national anthem.

The Star-Spangled Banner

Oh, say can you see by the dawn's early light
What so proudly we hailed at the twilight's last gleaming?
Whose broad stripes and bright stars thru the perilous fight,
O'er the ramparts we watched were so gallantly streaming?
And the rocket's red glare, the bombs bursting in air,
Gave proof through the night that our flag was still there.
Oh, say does that star-spangled banner yet wave
O'er the land of the free and the home of the brave?

JUG BAND ACOUSTICS

The music of jug bands evolved from African-American vaudeville performers in the South's urban areas, such as Memphis, Tennessee. Bands employed homemade instruments such as stoneware jugs played like wind instruments, metal spoons, comb kazoos, washboards, and gourd guitars. Mingled with traditional banjos and guitars, the energetic jug bands in the early 1900s were forerunners of the blues.

To play a traditional wind instrument like a trumpet or trombone, musicians blow air through their closed lips into a mouthpiece. Inside the instrument, air vibrates and shoots as a column into the resonator. The bell-shaped part at the front of the trumpet releases the sound as a musical note. By buzzing their lips across the rim of an open jug, musicians produce a variety of sounds.

MUSICAL NOTE

Contemporary jug bands perform toe-tapping country music using a wide variety of homemade instruments made from items found around the house.

- journal and pencil
- empty soda bottles
- water
- spoon

- **Investigate the physics of jug instruments.** Create your own jug instruments using soda bottles and water. Brainstorm some ideas. How will water levels in soda bottles impact the pitch and tone of the sound you make? Write out your theories.

- **Discover what kinds of tones and pitches you can produce by blowing into the bottles.** Can you play a song? What happens when you rap the bottles with a spoon? How does the sound change? What if you leave one empty?

- **If you play a brass instrument, you're already adept at creating sound with the embouchure.** Brass musicians alter lip tension and airflow to produce different sounds. Predict how you can apply the same technique to produce sounds on an empty bottle. Formulate a hypothesis and test it out. What about trying out different methods of buzzing your lips across the bottle's rim. Which positions result in higher and lower pitches? Can you play a song?

- **Demonstrate your jug-playing technique for a classmate, teacher, or family member.** Explain the physics of your sound production.

To investigate more, conduct your experiment with a stoneware or glass jug, such as an empty cider or milk jug. How do your results differ? Apply what you discovered in Warbling Wineglasses when you experimented with varying water levels to produce sounds of different pitches.

Chapter 4 ▶

The Roaring Twenties: Jazz, Blues, and Country

How did the growth of American cities influence music?

🎵 Some people objected to jazz as vulgar and inviting sinful behavior. But many young people in the nation's big cities loved the wild music and dancing that came with this exciting new American art form.

After the bloodshed of World War I, Americans entered an era of prosperity, artistic innovation, and fast living that came to be known as the Roaring Twenties. For the first time, there were more Americans living in cities than on farms. Unprecedented industrial growth and the large-scale availability of electricity, cars, telephones, radios, motion pictures, and a vast range of other new products doubled the total wealth in America during this time. The war was over, people had money in their pockets, and it was time for fun. And lots and lots of jazz.

The first commercial radio station hit the airways out of Pittsburg in 1920. Just three years later there were more than 500 stations in America and radios in more than 12 million homes. People were listening to music from their homes all across the country. In 1927, people bought 100 million phonograph records, which they played on crank-up Victrolas.

As people moved from the South to the industrial cities of the North, they brought along traditions of blues and jazz that originated in the fields of the Mississippi Delta and New Orleans. In an era of segregation, these historically African American music styles became mainstream, making music a powerful tool in the struggle against inequality.

BIRTH OF THE BLUES

When we think of the blues, we think of feeling down. Blues music deals with feelings of loss, misfortune, and grief, but at the same time it is about having fun and letting our troubles go. It shows us how to find joy in sadness and shed the blues.

From the end of the Civil War through the 1940s, many poor people in the South, both black and white, worked in fields as sharecroppers. Some sharecroppers were former slaves working land owned by their former masters. They put in long hours and barely made a living after paying their landlords for food, housing, and farm supplies.

By the 1920s, sharecroppers had developed their own rural field music that evolved from the field hollers, ballads, and work songs of slavery. All along the Mississippi River Delta, sharecroppers mingled on their front porches at night after a hard day's work. They held fiddle contests, played music, and tapped out juba rhythms on their bodies. Most were illiterate and could not read music, so they used verbal and musical improvisation. As they shared personal stories of hardship, lost loves, and social injustice, the music helped them to beat the blues and feel uplifted.

Notable Quotable

"New Orleans had a great tradition of celebration. Opera, military marching bands, folk music, blues, different types of church music, ragtime, echoes of traditional African drumming, and all of the dance styles that went with this music could be heard and seen throughout the city. When all of these kinds of music blended into one, jazz was born."

—Wynton Marsalis, jazz musician

PLAYLIST

Did you know "When the Saints Go Marching In" was originally an African American spiritual hymn? Check out how Louis Armstrong turned it into a jazz hit that has become the unofficial anthem of New Orleans.

MUSICAL NOTE

A flapper was a young woman in the 1920s who rebelled against the norms of the older generation. She wore short, bobbed hair and makeup, smoked cigarettes in public, and wore short skirts to dance to the energetic music of the Jazz Age.

The rhythms of the blues were taken from African drumming and played on guitar, banjo, harmonica, and later piano, sax, and trumpet. Musicians used their guitars to imitate human wails and shrieks. Together with moans, grunts, hollers, and other vocalizations, this created the sorrowful sounds that sparked the birth of the blues.

ALL THAT JAZZ

The lively sounds of jazz music that we know today emerged from the struggles of former slaves living in New Orleans. New Orleans style, or "Classic Jazz" started in the late 1800s and early 1900s with brass bands performing for parties and dances. Many of the musical instruments were salvaged from the Civil War, including the clarinet, saxophone, cornet, trombone, tuba, banjo, bass, guitar, and drums. It was a lively combination of ragtime, spirituals, marching tunes, and strong influences from the blues.

The earliest jazz musicians from New Orleans are not well known today. But when gravel-voiced Louis Armstrong (1901–1971) was discovered and first went to play in Chicago in 1922, jazz took off. His music was a collection of improvised solos around a structure. Improvisation is central to all jazz music, even when a musician is playing from printed music. A jazz tune might start out sounding like a slow, introspective blues song, but would then take off in unpredictable directions as musicians improvised and turned it into something entirely new.

JAZZ AND BLUES ON THE MOVE

Jazz and blues musicians flooded Chicago, Detroit, and other cities to escape segregation. For musicians heading north, Memphis, Tennessee, was an important stop along the Mississippi River. Blues musicians such as Memphis Minnie and Bessie Smith (1894–1937), the "Empress of the Blues," played to packed crowds at theaters on Beale Street in Memphis. By the end of the 1920s, Smith was the highest-paid black entertainer in the country, playing in sell-out theaters throughout the South, the North, and the Midwest.

Born McKinley Morganfield in Rolling Fork, Mississippi, Muddy Waters (1913–1983) grew up playing the blues harmonica and guitar in the swampy puddles of the Mississippi River. He eventually joined a traveling show and gained recognition.

Muddy Waters moved to Chicago in 1943 where he began playing in clubs and developed a style that gave an urban vibe to the rural Mississippi Delta blues. His hit single "Rollin' Stone" influenced the name of the major music magazine *Rolling Stone* and the famous rock band, the Rolling Stones. The electric blues sound of Muddy Waters made its way to England, and he became an international star who recorded with rock musicians well into the 1970s.

PLAYLIST

Listen to Bessie Smith singing the blues. Then listen to Janis Joplin (1943–1970) who reigned as the "Queen of Rock and Roll" In the late 1960s. Can you hear Bessie Smith's influence on Joplin's bluesy, raspy vocals and electric energy in her rock classic "Piece of My Heart?"

🎵 The blues flourished in Chicago with Muddy Waters, who is called the father of modern Chicago blues.

In Chicago, Louis Armstrong introduced the art of wordless, nonsense improvisation known as scat singing. Other bands from New Orleans made their way north and jazz spread to Europe as African American musicians flocked to Paris in search of cultural and creative freedoms.

Jazz became so popular in the 1920s that roadhouses filled with people kicking up their heels to its spontaneous sounds. They flocked to dance halls to hear jazz musicians and their big band orchestras. The Benny Goodman Orchestra at the Savoy in New York City and Duke Ellington at the Aragon in Chicago were sometimes joined by blues great Bessie Smith. Flappers danced new dances with names like the Black Bottom, Flea Hop, Cake Walk, and Charleston to the music of the big bands.

At the end of the decade, jazz began to take on a more free-flowing rhythm that became the trademark of the swing style of jazz. Early swing bands could have 16 or more instruments playing with and against each other. Hot bands like Count Basie's played quick, hard-driving tunes. Others like the Glen Miller Orchestra played slower, less improvised heartfelt songs. By the 1940s, solos were popular and band leaders became part of the orchestra, playing an instrument instead of conducting from the front. Dancers loved this music and a new swing style of dancing evolved.

COUNTRY AND WESTERN MUSIC

With chart-topping bands and artists including Lady Antebellum, Taylor Swift, Carrie Underwood, Garth Brooks, and Tim McGraw, country music enjoys a huge following. Like folk music and the blues, country is all about storytelling.

Country music evolved from European fiddling and African banjo playing, but it wasn't until the 1920s that country music took hold as a new genre of American music. Irish immigrants were among the first Europeans to settle in the southern Appalachian Mountains. Along with their beloved folk songs and ballads, the Irish brought their fiddles! This versatile instrument can swing from bouncy to melancholy. It inspires a range of emotions and was perfect for joyful jigs and reels as well as weepy ballads. People kicked up their heels to the fiddle's lively tunes and swayed to sorrowful ones.

The gourd banjos brought to the New World by slaves also inspired country music. African musicians covered bowl-like gourds with heads made from taut animal skin. Animal hair and plant fibers made heavy strings. These instruments probably produced low, mellow sounds. White folks in the South modified the instruments by crafting wooden banjos covered with groundhog-skin heads. By the mid-1800s, people played their fiddles and banjos together, laying the roots for country music and its offshoots.

In the early 1920s, artists like Fiddlin' John Carson, the Skillet Lickers, and Vernon Dalhart recorded some of country's first hits. WSN Radio's Grand Ole Opry began broadcasting live country music acts from Nashville, Tennessee, every Saturday night over the radio. And when Victor Records signed a recording contract with Mississippi native Jimmie Rogers in 1927, he became a major star with his release of "Blue Yodel #1," which sold over a million copies.

🎵 **Fiddle music was once called Old Time Music. As it developed into what we now call country and western, the genre kept its rural down-home sounds.**

MUSICAL NOTE

In 1925, Nashville's Grand Old Opry began weekly broadcasts of country music. With bluegrass, gospel, folk acts, and silly skits, the legendary show continues its run today. It has been instrumental in promoting country music artists ever since. You can listen to a live stream at www.opry.com/wsm/

🎵 **Because country music was often played on the same radio station as cowboy music, the term "country and western music" evolved.**

Listen to songs from several categories to experience the genre's different spins. Explore music from well-known country artists of the past and present.

bluegrass: Alison Kraus, Jimmy Martin, Dolly Parton, Earl Scruggs, Nitty Gritty Dirt Band

country and western: Hank Williams, Patsy Cline, Merle Haggard, Taylor Swift, Garth Brooks, Tim McGraw

cowboy: Gene Autry, Roy Rogers, Sons of the Pioneers

honky-tonk: Lefty Frizzell, Webb Pierce, Stonewall Jackson, Wanda Jackson

MUSICAL NOTE

Patsy Montana and her hit, "I Want to be a Cowboy's Sweetheart," led the way for women to have their own solo careers. Later many female Nashville Sound country artists recorded big hits, including Patsy Cline, Kitty Wells, Brenda Lee, and Loretta Lynn.

COWBOY MUSIC, BLUEGRASS, HONKY TONK, AND THE NASHVILLE SOUND

In the 1930s and '40s, cowboy movies popularized country music, which was sometimes called western music. People flocked to the movies to watch singing cowboy flicks on the big screen. Artists including Gene Autry, Roy Rogers, and Dale Evans crooned in clear, light tenor voices about life on the open range out West. String bands and harmonicas accompanied songs such as the Sons of the Pioneers's "Tumbling Tumble Weeds" and Gene Autry's "Cowboy Blues."

At the same time, Bill Monroe, Lester Flatt, and Earl Scruggs were spearheading the growth of bluegrass. This branch of country is known for its high, lonesome sound. Blended with English, Irish, Scottish, and Welsh traditional music and jazzy African-American flavors, bluegrass is infused with the sounds of stringed instruments. Like all other folk music, bluegrass rings with the spirit of the working class. Tunes such as "All Aboard" and "John Henry" told tales of hardscrabble times in railroad towns. "Sprinkle Coal Dust on My Grave" and "Dark as a Dungeon" lamented the treacherous jobs of Appalachian coal miners.

The 1950s brought another style of country music known as honky-tonk. At the time, a honky tonk was a bar located in a rural white southern community where people went to escape their difficult lives for a little while with live music. Sometimes called hillbilly, honky-tonk music embodies a spirit of working-class life, loneliness, drinking, and lost loves. Honky-tonk had its roots in the western swing style of country combined with jazz. The fiddle and the steel guitar feature in most of the songs, with stars such as Hank Williams, Lefty Frizzell, and Ernest Tubb.

In the late 1950s and '60s, a new country-pop Nashville Sound gained a large following, putting an end to the reign of honky-tonk. Nashville Sound combined country with the smooth sounds of popular jazz and swing bands of the day. Jim Reeves, Patsy Cline, and Eddy Arnold were the emotional, expressive crooners who brought this new, easy-listening country sound to larger audiences. They cemented country and western's place in American sound.

BLAST FROM THE PAST

Music has always brought people together. Bluegrass bands allowed folks to hang out and enjoy the music—and jump in for foot-stomping good times. Families and friends gathered on front porches and in homes. They stomped percussive Celtic clog dances. Watch these vintage clips. Take a look at the kids' vigorous clog dancing at a house party. Listen for the bouncy fiddle and bright banjo. Watch the Blue Ridge Mountain Dancers perform with Pete Seeger. Can you hear the buoyant fiddle and twangy banjo?

YIPPIE KI-YI YIPPIE-I A!

PICK A SOUND

Bluegrass music gets its distinctive sound from stringed instruments. Bluegrass musicians play fiddles, resonator guitars, upright basses, mandolins, and banjos. Stringed instruments produce sounds through the vibrations of strings in tension. The thickness and length of the strings determine the types of sounds produced. For example, a thin string produces a higher sound than a thick one. A loose string produces a lower sound than a tight one. How do different methods of playing impact sound?

Explore the way the sounds produced with the downward clawhammer style differ from the upward Scruggs style.

MUSICAL NOTE

The clawhammer is the oldest playing style. Slaves introduced this traditional style without picks, which many musicians use today.

- **First test out the clawhammer style.** Cup your hand like a claw against the banjo strings. Position all your fingers together. Keep the thumb separate, raised a bit above your fingers. Your hand will move in a downward direction. With a downstroke, strum a string, or strings, with your index and middle fingernails. Your thumb should catch strings, too. Experiment with the clawhammer until you feel comfortable with the style. Watch the way the strings vibrate as you strum down.

- **Now try the Scruggs style.** Slip on the thumb pick and cover your index and middle fingers with picks. Let your ring finger and pinky rest against the banjo head. Pluck upwards with the picks. The motion can be tricky. It requires dexterity.

- **Experiment with the Scruggs style until you are comfortable.** Some people find fingerpicks awkward. It might take extra practice to feel at ease. How do the strings vibrate as you play?

- **Record yourself playing a song or just noodling with both methods.** Listen to your recordings, and discuss your observations. How would you describe the sounds produced? How are they similar and different? Why do you think the two methods produce different sounds? What conclusions do you draw?

> To investigate more, use a flat pick to play the banjo. What differences do you hear in the sounds you produce? Why do you think they are different? Now use all of the styles you've learned to play some music.

Ideas for Supplies ▼

- journal and pencil
- five-string banjo or guitar
- fingerpicks
- flat picks
- computer with microphone

MUSICAL NOTE

Earl Scruggs (1924–2012) was a legendary bluegrass musician. Scruggs was renowned for his three-finger banjo style, today called the "Scruggs style." With picks on the thumb, index, and middle finger, Scruggs plucked upwards. Lightning-quick finger "rolls" created syncopated licks. His banjo banged out the driving beat of bluegrass. Watch Earl Scruggs's fantastic fingerpicking action with the classic instrumental, "Foggy Mountain Breakdown."

Chapter 5 ▶
War and Social Change: Patriotism and Protest

Do epic conflicts produce epic music?

The Roaring Twenties came to an end with the crash of the stock market in 1929 and the onset of the Great Depression. Gone was the exuberance and creative energy of the 1920s as people struggled to feed their families and keep their homes.

Over the following decades America became involved in large-scale military conflicts around the world. After the global conflict of World War II in the 1940s, came the battles against communism in Southeast Asia during the Korean and Vietnam Wars in the 1950s and 1960s. With the ups and downs of war, moods shifted from feelings of pride and unity to anger and dissention.

Some artists performed patriotic tunes to improve morale both on military bases and at home. But while America was united by a sense of working toward a common goal in World War II and the Korean War, the Vietnam War deeply divided the country. By the 1960s, many sang out with protest messages expressing anti-war sentiments.

At the same time, the civil rights movement was in full force during the 1960s and 1970s. As President Obama said during a Black History Month event in 2010, the civil rights movement was a movement sustained by music, lifted by spirituals, and sharpened by protest songs that sang of wrongs that needed righting.

WORLD WAR II, 1939–1945

Worldwide depression and lingering resentment in Europe after World War I paved the path for World War II. Germany invaded one country after another beginning in 1939. At first America stayed out of the war, but when Japan attacked Pearl Harbor in Hawaii on December 7, 1941, it stunned the military—and all Americans. More than 2,000 Americans died and another 1,000 were wounded at Pearl Harbor. The following day, President Franklin D. Roosevelt declared war on Japan. Within days, he declared war on Japan's allies, Germany and Italy. America entered the deadliest war in human history, a war that led to over 70 million civilian and military deaths worldwide.

On the home front, many supported World War II. People worked together to ration food and gas, plant victory gardens, and finance the war effort by buying War Bonds. News of the war came over the radio and through newspapers. There was universal heartbreak as families throughout the country lost fathers, brothers, cousins, and uncles.

As in past wars, music provided relief from the stresses of war. But World War II was the first in history to occur during an age of mass-distributed popular culture. Music was a shared experience. People huddled around radios to listen to tunes that rallied troops on the front and lifted spirits at home. They sang war songs and danced the jitterbug and the boogie-woogie.

BLAST FROM THE PAST

In 1905, composer-playwright George M. Cohan (1878–1942) wrote the rousing patriotic march "You're a Grand Old Flag" for the stage musical *George Washington, Jr.* It became the first American song from a stage musical to sell a million copies. The song is still a classic.

In the 1942 film *Yankee Doodle Dandy*, James Cagney portrayed George M. Cohan, who was one of the most talented song-and-dance men in Broadway history. Cagney used Cohan's technique of half-singing and half-reciting songs. Released during the early days of American involvement in World War II, the patriotic film inspired pride and unity. Cagney received an Academy Award for his role.

Written in 1941, the Andrews Sisters' three-part harmony, "Boogie Woogie Bugle Boy" became an iconic song of the era. The light-hearted jump blues song tells the story of a "famous trumpet man from out Chicago way" drafted for military duty who is stuck with a bugle, an instrument without valves. He's even more saddened that he only uses it to toot the wake-up reveille. His sympathetic captain quickly drafts a band to jam with the bugle boy and they entertain their company with bluesy rhythms! The happy story offered hope to troops about to depart for war.

THE GOLDEN AGE OF BROADWAY

These years were the golden age of Broadway. Many hits ran for over 1,000 shows. There's nothing like the in-the-moment experience of live theater. Musical theater is an American art form. The mark of success in American theater is a run in one of the 40 professional theaters in the Broadway district of Manhattan.

The seeds of Broadway were planted as early as 1750 when a theater holding nearly 300 people opened for Shakespearean productions and ballad operas. All theater stopped during the Revolutionary War but after the war, the Park Theater opened with 2,000 seats. More theaters opened as minstrel shows and vaudeville grew, and Broadway was an attractive place to build theaters in the 1800s because real estate prices were cheap.

The play *Show Boat* debuted in 1927, a popular musical set on a Mississippi River showboat based on a bestselling book. Critics and audiences loved the show. This was the launch of Broadway as the place for the best theater. The show ran for a year and a half, with a total of 572 performances.

In 1943, Roger's and Hammerstein's *Oklahoma* opened during the midst of World War II. Set in the early 1900s in the Indian Territory that became Oklahoma, it presented a simpler way of life and an escape from war's cruel realities. Combining song and dance numbers with dialogue, it was a smash, running for five years and 2,248 performances.

With enormous success, Oklahoma built off the success of Show Boat as a "book musical." Instead of musical numbers linked with snippets of dialogue and wacky gags, these musical plays feature integrated songs and dances. Performers portrayed genuine characters and audiences connected with their joys and sorrows.

THE VIETNAM WAR AND CIVIL RIGHTS MOVEMENT

Unlike World War II, which was nicknamed the "just war," the Vietnam War was an unpopular conflict among many Americans, especially young people. During the era's rapid cultural changes, a generation gap split kids and parents. Kids rebelled against their parents' ways of life. A counterculture rose up to spread messages of peace and love.

Flashing peace signs and wearing strands of love beads, young people known as hippies took to the streets. They were committed to nonviolent protest and opposed the war. Their shocked parents had endured the hardships of the Great Depression and the sorrows of World War II. Many were patriotic veterans. They didn't understand their kids' behavior and their kids didn't understand why. Bridging the gap seemed hopeless.

Steven Van Zandt of the E Street Band lived the generation gap. He told _Time_ magazine, "It's one of the few times in history where it was the dramatic shift between the past and the future, where the parents could not relate to the children."

In 1964, folksinger-songwriter and social activist Bob Dylan (1941–) sang "The Times They are a-Changin'." The anthem's lyrics, concerning issues of racism, poverty, and social change, still resonate:

The order is rapidly fadin'

And the first one now will later be the last

For the times they are a-changin'.

As the Vietnam War escalated and Dylan released his song, unrest gripped the nation. A disproportionate number of African Americans were drafted into the Vietnam War. Most of them experienced combat. A mass civil rights movement took a stand against segregation and discrimination in the South. As the 1960s rolled on, the women's rights movement gained momentum as well.

Musicians from all musical genres embraced the spirit of revolution. Protesters marched on Washington and belted out powerful hymns, including the freedom song "We Shall Overcome," which became the theme song of the civil rights movement. White folk artists, including Pete Seeger, Bob Dylan, Joan Baez, Janis Ian, and Phil Ochs sang of the shame of segregation and racism.

Jazz was so bound together with the civil rights movement that Martin Luther King delivered the opening address to the Berlin Jazz Festival in Berlin, Germany, in 1964. "Jazz speaks for life," King said. "The blues tell the story of life's difficulties—and, if you think for a moment, you realize that they take the hardest realities of life and put them into music, only to come out with some new hope or sense of triumph. This is triumphant music."

MOTOWN: HITSVILLE USA

Launched during the Civil Rights movement, the legendary Motown record label was the first label owned by an African American. It became a powerful source of cultural and social change, promoting black artists to mainstream, mostly white audiences. Motown Sound was uplifting and upbeat. With a blend of jazz, gospel, and traditional call-and-response, it introduced soul music to a mass audience.

Singer-songwriter Berry Gordy, Jr. (1928–) borrowed $800 from his family in 1959 and used it to turn his small Detroit home into a hit-making factory. The garage was the recording studio and the kitchen was the control station.

It didn't take Gordy long to sign his first group, Smokey Robinson and the Miracles. By 1961, the Miracles released Motown's first million-copy seller, "Shop Around." And the year kept getting better. The teen girl group, the Marvelettes, released "Please, Mr. Postman," which became Motown's first *Billboard* Hot 100 single and was later covered by The Beatles in 1963. With the Temptations' hit song "My Girl," and the Supremes' "Where Did Our Love Go?" Motown was officially mainstream. In 1968 the company had five records out of the Top 10 on *Billboard*'s Hot 100 chart.

Motown's upbeat sound united black and white, old and young. Diana Ross was the admiration of all teenage girls and the boys wanted to be just like Smokey Robinson. In the late '80s and '90s, all of Motown's major artists were inducted into the Rock and Roll Hall of Fame. When Gordy himself was inducted in 1988, he was given the following tribute: "Gordy endeavored to reach across the racial divide with music that could touch all people, regardless of the color of their skin." And he did just that.

How did Gordy come up with the name Motown? He replaced the "city" in Detroit's "Motor City" nickname with the more folksy, "town" to reflect his warm feelings about his community. Motor Town was soon shortened to Motown.

MUSICAL NOTE

It's no surprise Motown earned the nickname Hitsville USA. The label cranked out more than 180 No. 1 hits. Its stellar artists included Diana Ross and the Supremes, Smokey Robinson and the Miracles, Stevie Wonder, the Temptations, the Four Tops, Marvin Gaye, Michael Jackson and the Jackson 5, and Lionel Richie and the Commodores.

GET YOUR GROOVE ON! GRAVITY AND BALANCE IN DANCE

During World War II, dancing provided entertainment and an escape from the grim realities of the time. Dance is an art form, but physics is behind the moves! A force is a push or pull on an object. Gravity is one force that acts on all dancers to keep them balanced when they're in motion. Gravity pushes down on a dancer while the floor beneath the dancer's feet pushes up. How do dancers stay balanced? With subtle body shifts and adjustments. You can test a variety of body positions as you explore gravity and balance.

- **Consider some questions to explore**. You might consider: To stay balanced, where should your center of gravity be positioned? Will it be harder to balance if your feet are close together over a small section of the floor, or wider apart over a larger area? How should the body shift and adjust to stay balanced on one leg positioned to the back? To the front? When leaping? When spinning? Make predictions and formulate a hypothesis.

OOF!

- **Decide what types of moves to test, and list them in the Move Executed portion of the data chart.** For example, you might test spins, leaps, and kicks.

- **Get your move on!** Take turns testing and spotting. The spotter should stand close enough to help if necessary but not too close to be an obstruction. As you test each move, note the position of your arms and legs. Measure the area you covered to execute the move. How did you make adjustments to stay balanced—or not. Dancers take tumbles all the time, even trained pros. Draw a simple diagram to illustrate body positions. What can you conclude from your tests? Evaluate your hypothesis.

Ideas for Supplies

- journal and pencil
- yardstick or tape measure
- computer

Move Executed	
Position of Arms	
Position of Legs	
Area Covered	
Adjustments	
Diagram	

To investigate more, use a computer choreography program to create diagrams of dance moves. Use your discoveries and diagrams to choreograph a dance.

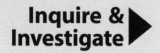

BOOGIE WOOGIE BUGLE

Tweens and teens in the 1940s jitterbugged to the cheery "Boogie Woogie Bugle Boy" of the Andrews Sisters. What kinds of sounds can you produce with your own bugle?

With your classmates, teacher, or parent, design an instrument. Explore the sounds you can produce with a bugle constructed of a length of garden hose and a funnel. Experiment with posture, breathing, and lip vibrations.

- **Before you begin construction, sketch a design.** Loop a section of hose in different ways to find a position that's comfortable for you to hold and maintain. Indicate where you will duct tape the hose in place. Note the funnel size you will use to create a bell at the end of the bugle. The larger the funnel, the louder the sound your instrument will produce. It's like a megaphone to amplify and spread notes. You will also need a mouthpiece. A soda bottle spout cut off the bottle works well. Can you think of other ways to make a mouthpiece?

- **Construct your bugle.** Duct tape works well to hold all the pieces together. What color duct tape did you choose? Do you want to decorate your bugle in any way?

- **Experiment with posture.** How does your bugle sound when you stand or sit straight and tall? How does it sound if you stand or sit in more scrunched-up positions? Try pressing your lips to the mouthpiece with different amounts of pressure. What makes the cleanest sounds?

- **Now, the trick is to buzz your lips to produce a sound like a "bzzz bee!"** If you're a brass player, demonstrate for others. You'll need to keep your lips moist to produce sounds—and that will collect saliva in the mouthpiece. Shake and wipe out the mouthpiece as needed. Your lips' vibrations will send a column of air into the bugle and out the bell to produce sound.

> To investigate more, design and construct bugles with funnels of different sizes. If you have a trumpet mouthpiece, test it. How do the sounds you produce differ and compare? Learn to play the reveille call or "Boogie Woogie Bugle Boy." Play along with other tunes, and invite other musicians to jam.

Ideas for Supplies

- journal and pencil
- old garden hose
- knife
- plastic soda bottle
- funnel
- duct tape
- cloth to wipe out bell

KALEIDOSCOPIC EXTRAVAGANZA

During the 1920s, Busby Berkeley was a dance director for a number of Broadway musicals in which he arranged dancers into attractive geometric patterns. Throughout the 1930s and 1940s, he gained fame for creating spectacular human kaleidoscopic extravaganzas. A kaleidoscope is an optical device that uses reflected light to create dazzling symmetrical patterns.

What makes an object symmetrical? When it has the exact reflection on opposite sides of a dividing line. Consider rotational symmetry. If you rotate an object around a center point, at any angle from 0 to 360 degrees, presto! The object matches itself several times as it rotates. That's what happens as you spin a kaleidoscope.

Explore light's properties and the effects that angled mirrors create as you observe rotational symmetry with a homemade kaleidoscope.

🎵 **Order of symmetry refers to the number of times an object looks the same in rotation. An object with no symmetry, like the letter R, is an order one. It must spin a full 360 degrees before it looks the same. An order two object is rotated halfway, to 180 degrees. Try it out. Write a large X on a sheet of paper. Draw a line of axis through it. Fold the paper lengthwise to the right along the axis, then lengthwise to the left. The X's halves should match both times because they are mirror images.**

- **Before you begin construction, sketch a diagram for your own simple device.** You will want the three mirrors lengthwise with the reflecting sides facing inward. How can you attach them securely to form an equilateral triangle? A piece of wax paper at the bottom of the triangle makes a screen to look through. Arrange some shiny items on the white cardboard and hold the kaleidoscope above it to view them.

- **Observe rotational symmetry.** Sketch some of the designs. What happens as you rotate the mirrors? How many images do you observe? What happens when you rearrange the shiny items, or add different ones?

To investigate more, experiment with choreography. Use the sketches you created for inspiration. How can you orchestrate a kaleidoscopic arrangement like Busby Berkeley? View a Busby Berkeley production number from an old film. Watch a clip from the movie *Gold Diggers* of 1933. How are dancers arranged symmetrically? How does the whirling stage make moves kaleidoscopic? How does the camera angle allow the viewer to observe the beauty of symmetry?

Can you choreograph your friends or family members to use symmetrical arm and leg action to form images? Trying using props such as fans and feathers!

Ideas for Supplies

- journal and pencil
- 3 flat, rectangular mirrors
- transparent tape
- rubber bands
- shiny items such as foil confetti, sequins, beads
- white cardboard

BLAST FROM THE PAST

The Beatles sang of a girl with kaleidoscope eyes in their 1967 classic "Lucy in the Sky With Diamonds." What's the story behind the ethereal music? Lucy O'Donnell was the song's famed Lucy. She attended Heath House nursery school with Julian Lennon (1963–), the son of singer-songwriter John Lennon (1940–1980).

At the age of four, Julian created a drawing of his pal. Julian showed his artwork to his dad and announced, "That's Lucy in the sky with diamonds." The artwork ignited a flame of inspiration in the musician.

CHANGIN' TIMES:
SONGS OF SOCIAL PROTEST

Some protest songs of the Vietnam and civil rights era issued calls to action for social justice. Others, like the spirituals that preceded them, shared consolation and comfort. Many consider Bob Dylan's 1963 "Blowin' in the Wind" to be the most important protest song ever written. The song's melody borrows from the slavery-era folk song "No More Auction Block for Me." The lyrics pose questions about freedom, peace, and war, suggesting that things must and will change.

Listen to some protest songs and identify their themes and messages. Interpret the lyrics and determine whether each song is a call to action, a consolation, or an encouragement. Or does it contain another message?

Notable Quotable

"Deep in my heart, I do believe, we shall overcome."

—Dr. Martin Luther King, Jr., (1929–1968) in a brief speech just four days before his assassination in March 1968

- **What are some features to listen for in the songs?** Jot down your ideas.

- **Listen to and evaluate the songs in the data chart.** Can you find other protest songs to add to your list?

- **Share your observations about the songs and discuss the lyrics you noted.** What conclusions can you draw?

Song Title	Artist	Song's Purpose(s)	Evidence in Lyrics
We Shall Overcome	Pete Seeger		
We Shall Overcome	Joan Baez		
Blowin' in the Wind	Bob Dylan		
A Change is Gonna Come	Sam Cooke		
Keep on Pushing	The Impressions		
What's Going On	Marvin Gaye		

To investigate more, think about the ways the songs of the past can be applied to issues of today. How do the lyrics still resonate? What tweaks would you make in the lyrics to update them and call attention to a specific issue of the moment?

BLAST FROM THE PAST

Aretha Franklin (1942–) recorded "Respect" in 1967, which shot to the top of both the R&B and pop charts. Known as the Queen of Soul, her rendition of "Respect" was called the civil rights and feminist anthem of the time, symbolizing an appeal for respect and dignity. She sang the hymn "Precious Lord, Take My Hand" at Martin Luther King, Jr.'s funeral in 1968. More than 40 years later in 2009, Franklin sang "My Country 'Tis of Thee," a patriotic hymn written in 1831, at President Barack Obama's inauguration.

MUSICAL NOTE

The Temptations were also known for their sharp suits, smooth voices, and precision dance moves that included elegant and synchronized kicks, slides, and turns.

PLAYLIST

Visit the Motown Museum online. Explore the unforgettable Motown Sound. How about giving the Four Tops, Stevie Wonder, and the Temptations a spin? Listen to Motown's fantastic girl groups Diana Ross and the Supremes, Martha and the Vandellas, and the Marvelettes. Where do you hear influences of gospel and jazz? Which songs feature a call-and-response pattern?

SING IN HARMONY

Motown artists the Temptations earned great success in the 1960s and '70s. Many consider them R&B and soul's most influential performers. One of the most successful bands ever, the Temptations boasted epic vocal harmonies that have sold tens of millions of records.

Work with your classmates, friends, or family members to explore vocal harmony.

- **Experiment with vocal ranges as you sing a series of octaves.** Who can sing at the highest, middle, and lowest pitch? Is there someone who can use the keyboard to establish the appropriate pitch for each note?

- **Try a simple song, such as "Frère Jacques" or "Twinkle, Twinkle Little Star."** Sing in a parallel style. Invite the person with the middle pitch to sing the main melody. Blend your voices as you sing simultaneously. The voice taking on upper harmony sings one full octave above the middle pitch. The lower-harmony voice sings one full octave below. That way, voices will sound clearly different—and that creates harmony. If full octave differences aren't sung, the pitches won't be distinct and the sound can get muddled.

- **Record yourselves as you harmonize.** Listen to the playback, and assess your sound. Where do you need to make tweaks? What sounds great? Why? Can you make improvements? Record yourselves again and compare the two versions.

Ideas for Supplies ▼

- journal and pencil
- keyboard
- computer
- recording equipment

To investigate more, watch a performance of the Temptations beloved soul classic "My Girl" and listen to the incredible three-part harmony.

- Listen to the amazing arrangement of voices. David Ruffin sings lead in a sweet, smooth melody. The rest of the group tackles harmonic background vocals. When can you hear the lowest voice come in? The highest voices? How do all voices combine and blend? What impact does harmony have on the song?

- How does the chorus, "My girl, my girl, my girl/ Talkin' 'bout my girl/My girl" use harmony? How does harmony add emphasis to the meaning?

- Share your observations. Then, watch the performance again. Sing along with the Temptations. Choose one person to sing melody and the others to provide back up. Practice singing with your different pitches to combine your voices. Record your rehearsals and critique your sound.

Chapter 6 ▶
Rock and Roll Is Here to Stay

What makes rock
music so popular?

In 1951, disc jockey Alan Freed began playing rhythm and blues music for a multi-racial audience in Cleveland, Ohio. He is credited with first using the phrase "rock and roll" to describe the music.

BLAST FROM THE PAST

Billboard Magazine started ranking the top singles in the music industry in 1948 and has published their rankings every week since. They look at how often the song is played on the radio or how many copies are sold. Today, they also factor in song streaming from the Internet.

In 2012, Americans made a record number of music purchases. What type of music did they choose the most? Rock! Topping the charts at over 102 million albums sold, even the next-closest type was still a subgenre of rock called "alternative," which sold 52.2 million albums.

Though today's rock sounds different from what first emerged in the 1950s, generations of artists have impacted the rock music you listen to today. Rock's guitar-jamming, piano-banging, sax-wailing pioneers, including Chuck Berry, Jerry Lee Lewis, Fats Domino, Little Richard, and Elvis, electrified audiences and influenced those that followed. With roots in blues, country, gospel, and R&B, rock and roll promises something for all tastes. Teenagers across racial, religious, and social lines all find a place in rock's eclectic universe.

Since about 1967, the term "rock" has been used to describe not only classic rock music itself, but also its many related styles, including rockabilly, folk rock, hard rock, soft rock, punk rock, and heavy metal.

THE BIRTH OF ROCK AND ROLL

After World War II, a youth culture emerged. Nearly 80 million babies were born between 1946 and 1964. This was the Baby Boomer generation and the era's kids hungered for music to call their own. Rock and roll careened onto the stage in the prosperous post-war era and its exhilarating hook never let go!

Baby Boomers claimed rock as their own. They were the first generation to grow up to the rhythms of rock and to grow up with TV. New forms of mass media meant rockers could get their music out to an enormous national audience. Kids listened to music on the radio, bought rock 'n roll records, watched *American Bandstand* in the afternoon, and went to movies featuring rock and roll music. Watching bands on TV became as popular as spinning vinyl on record players and cranking transistor radios. When people watched thrilling new artists on TV, the next day the same catchy tunes were "stuck" in millions of heads.

As rock evolved in the 1960s and 1970s, musicians navigated the rapidly changing times. The music they played reflected the conflicts young people had with an older generation, with society, and with the world.

What's behind rock's incredible staying power? It challenges each of us to explore our own role in society. Much of rock music's emotional power comes from its reflection of the search for who we are. Songwriters and artists strive to define themselves through their music and to inspire us to question the world around us and formulate personal beliefs.

PLAYLIST

Listen to songs from many types of rock music to understand how broad the category of rock is. With your parents, or with their permission, explore music from these well-known artists.

- **rockabilly**: Johnny Cash and Elvis Presley, Little Richard

- **folk rock**: Bob Dylan and Simon & Garfunkel

- **hard rock**: Led Zeppelin and the Who

- **soft rock**: Carol King and Cat Stevens

- **punk rock**: The Clash and the Ramones

- **heavy metal**: Metallica and Kiss

🎵 *American Bandstand* **was a popular show that ran from 1952 until 1989. It broadcasted teen styles, tastes, and music across the United States.**

♪ "Rock Around the Clock" became the first rock and roll single to top the *Billboard* charts. Over 25 million copies have been sold around the world.

Notable Quotable

"If you tried to give rock and roll another name, you might call it 'Church Berry.'"

—John Lennon, The Beatles

PLAYLIST

In 1974, the popular TV show *Happy Days* used "Rock Around the Clock" as its theme song and introduced the tune to a new generation of kids. Decades later, reruns of the popular show keep "Rock Around the Clock" rolling.

CHUCK BERRY

In the late 1940s and early 1950s, R&B's strong backbeat, driving 4/4 time, and 12-bar blues laid tracks for rock and roll's rollout. In those days, kids listened to rock secretly, when parents weren't around. But by 1955, things looked very different.

Chuck Berry's (1926–) influence on rock and roll could be the greatest of all the early breakthrough rock and roll artists. Brian Wilson of the Beach Boys said, he wrote "all of the great songs and came up with all the rock & roll beats." Recorded in 1955, Berry's first single, "Maybellene" featured imaginative lyrics, a 24-bar guitar solo in the middle, and a thumping beat. It was promoted by disc jockey Alan Freed and embraced by white teenagers. His rock and roll classics, which include "Roll Over Beethoven," "Johnny B. Goode," and "Rock and Roll Music" have been covered by a wide range of artists, such as Elvis Presley, the Beatles, the Rolling Stones, the Beach Boys, Jimi Hendrix, and Bruce Springsteen.

BILL HALEY AND THE COMETS

In 1954, Bill Haley and the Comets released their exuberant, raucous single, "Rock Around the Clock." When the song was featured in the 1955 film *Blackboard Jungle*, it kicked up a frenzy that launched the rock revolution. A celebration of music and dance with a rockabilly beat, the song's lyrics boasted an unforgettable hook that foreshadowed rock's continuing popularity:

We're gonna rock around the clock tonight

We're gonna rock, rock, rock, 'till broad daylight

We're gonna rock, gonna rock around the clock tonight.

THE KING—ELVIS PRESLEY

This entertainment icon was one of the most popular artists of the twentieth century. He only needs one name—Elvis—and millions of people know exactly who it is. Elvis Presley (1935–1977), nicknamed "The King," has sold over 1 billion records worldwide.

Deeply influenced by gospel music, Elvis' energetic, uninhibited style embraced the joy of rock and delivered it to a larger audience. He fused several styles by vigorously blending southern folk music, country, and rock and roll. When it was "all shook up," he helped spread rockabilly to the masses.

To some people, Elvis represented the generation gap. Many blamed him for coming between kids and adults. Younger audiences swooned for Elvis' swagger and swivel-hipped dance moves that shocked their parents. With a slicked pompadour, a hairdo with a swirl over the forehead, and a rockabilly strut, he was a living, breathing symbol of what kids loved and parents feared. Preachers denounced Elvis from their pulpits and smashed his records.

BLAST FROM THE PAST

Like Elvis, Bill Haley and the Comets also made historic appearances on *The Ed Sullivan Show*. The weekly variety program that ran from 1948 to 1971 proved instrumental in helping new talent gain recognition.
Early rock and roll legends, including Little Richard, Chuck Berry, the Beatles, and the Rolling Stones connected with millions of far-flung fans when they appeared on the show.

In the late 1960s, Janis Joplin (1943–1970) reigned as the "Queen of Rock and Roll." Her bluesy, raspy vocals and electric energy drove the rock classic "Piece of My Heart." Florence Welch (1986–), lead singer of indie rockers Florence and the Machine, studied videos of Joplin's wailing performances. Can you see and hear influences of Joplin in Welch's video of "Dog Days are Over?" Welch said, "Her connection with the audience was really important. It seems to me the suffering and intensity of her performance go hand in hand. There was always a sense of longing, of searching for something. I think she really sums up the idea that soul is about putting your pain into something beautiful. And that's why she's so important to me."

In 1956, Elvis gave an electrifying performance to 60 million people of all ages who tuned in to watch him on *The Ed Sullivan Show*. He belted out "Don't Be Cruel," crooned "Love Me Tender," and closed with "Hound Dog." As parents pushed back against rock even more, Elvis became more loved among millions of teenagers.

THE BRITISH INVASION

In the mid-1960s, music from British rock and roll bands spread to the United States and gave birth to a new age of rock.

By 1963, the Beatles had taken Britain by storm. That December, the single "I Want to Hold Your Hand" spent seven weeks as number 1 on the charts in the United States. When they came to New York in February 1964, 73 million people watched them on *The Ed Sullivan Show*. Two other British bands, the Rolling Stones and the Who, also became wildly popular.

Rolling Stone magazine named the Who's 1965 hit "My Generation" the 11th greatest song of all time. "My Generation" became an anthem of the generation gap.

Featuring a call-and-response, lead vocalist Roger Daltry sang, "People try to put us d-down," while Pete Townsend and John Entwhistle harmonized on backups, "Talkin' 'bout my generation."

THE 1970s AND BEYOND

The widespread move for change during the Vietnam War produced some of the era's best rock. Kids flocked to record stores to snag hot new releases. At home, they blasted vinyl on record players and stereos. After the war, a mix of hard rock and blues created a new sound made popular by Queen, the Eagles, David Bowie, Yes, and Led Zeppelin. Late in the 1970s, The Ramones combined teenage rage with rock and roll to launch the next huge movement in rock as punk music took center stage.

Generation X, the 46 million born from 1964 to 1980, hit their teen years in the 1980s and '90s. Gen-X rocked out to such an eclectic variety of sounds, it's hard to characterize the '80s by any one form of music. Heavy metal bands such as Guns and Roses, Van Halen, AC/DC, and Aerosmith took hold with their power ballads and wailing guitar solos. A punk, funk, disco mix called "new wave" was made popular by the B-52s, Talking Heads, and Blondie. Indie and alternative rock came along later in the decade with the Cure, R.E.M., and U2, and was the music of choice in Gen-X college dormitories. Expression of teenage angst continued in the 1990s when the Seattle grunge band Nirvana belted out their dark lyrics over strong guitar riffs with distortion and feedback.

While rock is one of the newer styles of music, its variety has given it the broadest appeal. Almost every rock band around today was influenced by rock and roll's true pioneers. If you haven't listened to a good Beatles song lately, you're missing out!

The word "indie" stands for independent and refers to diverse musicians and bands that are part of independent record labels. Popular on university radio stations, indie music is often called college rock.

MUSICAL NOTE

Patti Smith (1946–) is nicknamed the "Godmother of Punk." With passionate, poetic rock, the raw-voiced singer created compelling visual images through words. Her most widely known song, "Because the Night" reached number 13 on the charts in 1978. In *She's a Rebel: The History of Women in Rock and Roll*, Gillian G. Gaar writes, "Smith's biting delivery was something new for a female singer." Her audiences remain fanatically loyal.

PEOPLE HAVE THE POWER

Whether in protest songs or pure rock and roll, a song's lyrics implore us to consider the mood and issues of the day. They explore political, social, and religious identities. You can also use music to explore who you are.

- **Listen to the tunes on the Playlist here and others of your choice.** Some people respond to angry songs, while others prefer those that are gentle. Interpret the lyrics and evaluate different styles. What issues do the songs address? What emotions does the music stir? How do artists' voices and delivery styles impact their messages? Identify an issue facing the country or your own community today.

PLAYLIST

Rocker Bruce Springsteen's (1949–) classic "Born in the USA" is a passionate expression of the difficulties Vietnam War veterans faced when they returned home after serving their country.

U2's "Sunday, Bloody, Sunday." With its anguished tone and militaristic beat, it recalls the 1976 incident in Derry, Ireland, in which British police shot civil rights protesters.

Pete Seeger's mournful anti-war song, "Where Have All the Flowers Gone?"

Punk rocker and political activist Patti Smith's "People Have the Power," an optimistic song for hope.

- **Use it as a theme for an original composition.** Decide what kind of approach you will take—dreamy, defiant, sarcastic, serious, humorous, etc. You can present your composition as a poem, or set it to music.

To investigate more, listen to a variety of songs that address the quest for identity. Can you find common themes and messages? Listen to and evaluate lyrics from:

- "Just a Girl," which addresses female stereotypes, written by No Doubt's Gwen Stefani and Tom Dumont.

- "Waiting for My Real Life to Begin," which expresses a yearning for the future, by Colin Hay.

- "Still Haven't Found What I'm Looking For," a seeking song by U2.

Can you make a personal connection to the songs? Are there any songs that express similar feelings or questions you've experienced?

Compose a song about who you are or your own search to define yourself. Brainstorm issues you are passionate about. What contributions would you like to make to the world, big or small? What are your hopes and dreams for the future? Generate a word cloud to capture your ideas. Use it for inspiration. Write at least three verses with a chorus. Include a melodious hook to snag your listener's attention.

Notable Quotable

"Imagine all the people sharing all the world."

—John Lennon, "Imagine"

ROCKIN' ROBIN

Birds are nature's rock and roll musicians! With your teacher, classmates, or family, conduct a field study. Take a nature hike, and listen to the melodies of beautiful birdsongs. Record birdsongs and use them in an original composition. Can you duplicate the sounds with your own voice or with a musical instrument?

- **Consider questions such as the following: What are the rhythms of their sounds?** How do birds use pitch? How do birds respond to other calls? Discuss your ideas, and brainstorm additional questions. Make predictions. What methods and devices can you use to record birdsongs?

- **In the field, scout for multiple quiet locations where you can listen to birdsongs and make recordings.** Do you hear any other sounds, such as a woodpecker rapping against a tree trunk or the flapping of a great blue heron's wings? How are the sounds rhythmic? How can you use them as a backbeat?

- **After your field study, how can you analyze your data and evaluate your results?** Experiment with musical instruments and your voice to duplicate birdsongs. Arrange your recordings into an original composition. You can also upload recordings into a composition and notation program.

- **Rehearse your piece with your group and perform it for an audience.** Can audience members identify nature's influence?

BLAST FROM THE PAST

In 1958, R&B vocalist Bobby Day (1932–1990) topped the charts with "Rockin' Robin," by Leon René. The hit single's driving rhythm and bright, buoyant lyrics featured a catchy, "Tweedle-lee-dee-dee-dee" lead-in.

* science journal
  and pencil
* recording
  devices
* musical
  instruments
* music
  composition
  and notation
  software

To investigate more, explore an online source such as xeno-canto.org. This citizen science project shares worldwide birdsongs. Can you identify the birdsongs you heard, or confirm the species you listened to? View and listen to Bobby Day's 1958 performance of "Rockin' Robin." How does the song use a robin's chirruping and tweeting? Which instruments provide the birdsong? Check out the Jackson Five's 1972 cover of the same song. Which version more effectively employs the birdsong, and why? Compose and perform a hip-hop cover of "Rockin' Robin."

Chapter 7
The Age of Technology

How has digital technology changed music?

🎵 Hip-hop is widely popular in the United States, with artists including Jay Z, Eminem, Lil Wayne, Nicki Manaj, Eve, and Fergie topping the charts.

Today you live in an uber-connected world where the pace of new technology is daily news. The Millennial Generation includes 78 million people born from 1981 to 2000. In a generation still growing, kids born from 2001 to the present are described as Generation Z. These generations are the most racially and ethnically diverse in American's history.

Technology is an essential part of everyday life for these generations. These are kids like you who have grown up with text messaging, blogs, social networking, and more. With a swipe or a tap, you're connected. You can record a song and text it to a friend across town. Or shoot a video to send to a relative halfway around the world. You can download the music and watch the performances included in this book.

When did technology's incredible influence on the music scene amp up? Toward the end of the twentieth century, with rock's continued popularity and the birth of hip-hop. You may not remember a time before downloads, but that's when hip-hop began.

HIP-HOP'S FATHER

In 1973, a girl turning 16 wanted to raise money to buy clothes before starting school. She rented the recreation room of her apartment building and threw a party. Her brother, Clive Campbell, and his record collection provided the music. Three hundred people came to her "DJ Kool Herc Party," and everyone had a great time. By the next summer, Clive Campbell was playing outdoors at parks and in clubs in the Bronx. He started experimenting with two turntables and two copies of the same record, focusing on percussion and playing the drum sections of the albums one after the other. Vocals and other instruments were dropped out, creating a beat that people loved to dance to. At the same time he recited rhymes.

DJ Kool Herc (1955–) is the stage name of Jamaican-born artist Clive Campbell. He's a legend, and the father of hip-hop. In 1973, he began blasting a thrilling new genre into the music scene of New York from the streets of the Bronx. Campbell's family had immigrated from Jamaica where a sound system culture of technology created mobile discothéques of turntables, massive speakers, and charismatic DJs.

Like so many other immigrants, from colonial times to the present, Campbell transferred cultural memories to a new home. With roving dance clubs, Jamaican DJs shared American soul and R&B music along with their traditional reggae music. Toasting was a tradition in Jamaica. This chanting, or talking over a rhythm or beat, directly influenced hip-hop.

🎵 Hip-hop music is the stylized rhythmic music that forms the background for rapping. Hip-hop culture is defined by rapping, DJing and scratching, break dancing, slam poetry, and beatboxing.

Hip-hop evolved from West African griot traditions brought to America by slaves. West African griots were wandering poets, storytellers, and musicians who shared traditional tales and sounds through the oral tradition.

MUSICAL NOTE

When freestyle rappers like Eminem and Jay-Z spit rhymes off the top of their heads, neuroscientists discovered that the brain's prefrontal cortex is hard at work. That's the portion of the brain that controls our drive and motivation. They also saw that the portions that act as our inner critic shuts off, letting our creative juices flow. When you create, turn off that pesky inner critic. Get lost in your creative energy. Get in the flow!

LIVE STREET PERFORMANCE

Hip-hop expanded throughout the 1970s, although it still remained contained in New York. At that time, rap was called emceeing. Artists performed live at massive block parties. At these raucous street celebrations, MCs were the opening acts for DJs, who provided the main attraction with scratching. Using their hands, DJs zigzagged vinyl LPs over turntables. It was a bold innovation. With a screech that demanded attention, scratching literally turned the tables on recorded music. It challenged people to listen up and reimagine rhythms.

Soon, the performing tables turned when the MCs seized center stage and DJs provided background accompaniment. MCs performed to the consistent beat of instrumentals, while DJs arranged compositions.

What is behind a rapper's rhythmic delivery and witty vocals? Storytelling pulses at the heart of hip-hop with stories that grab the listener. Like the wandering balladeers, spiritual singers, blues musicians, and protest singers who came before them, rappers have something to say. Audiences latched onto their messages of the struggles and difficulties of living in poverty in the inner cities, and the anger and sadness of social inequalities.

RAPID CHANGES

Kurt Walker (1959–) uses the stage name Kurtis Blow. In 1979, with his influence, rap exploded out of the underground scene. Hip-hop went mainstream when Blow became the first rapper signed to a record label, Mercury Records.

Collaborating with other pioneers, including Grandmaster Flash, Mele Mel, and Russell Simmons, Blow was the first rapper to go on a national and international concert tour. His 1980 song "The Breaks" hit gold. The musical melting pot of hip-hop flourished with mass media distribution in the same way rock did. By 1981, visuals and sound combined in the popular music videos kids watched on MTV. In 1982, the digital revolution brought CD players. Listeners played any genre on portable CDs as well as cassettes and vinyl. By 1998, music lovers were exploring the new technology of MP3 players.

The world seemed a hopeful place at the start of the new millennium. But radical changes and heartbreak came with the devastating terrorist attacks on the World Trade Center on September 11, 2001. By the end of 2008, millions had lost homes in the housing crisis. People struggled to find work in a dwindling job market while wars in Iraq and Afghanistan dragged on and on. Once again, music offered an escape and helped rally people for action.

Kids found refuge in music—and connectivity. They turned away from listening to music on the radio. They stopped browsing old-school records shops, because listeners could find access at their fingertips. By 2011, 45 million people paid for music downloads through services like iTunes, Pandora, Rdio, and Spotify. In 2013, Twitter's 20 million users gained access to Twitter #music, an amazing service that highlights hot tracks and emerging artists. As Twitter noted, "And, of course, you can tweet songs right from the app."

In 2012, alternative singer-songwriter Beck released an unusual collection. *Song Reader* is a book of original songs written by Beck, but it includes only the sheet music. It is not a recorded album. You buy the book of music and the rest is up to you. It's a blast from the past when, as the innovative artist said, "The idea of sitting around a piano and playing a song with your friends and family was as much a part of our consciousness as Facebook is now." Musicians can post their own performances of the songs to the *Song Reader* official website. Renditions range from acoustic guitar instrumental versions to synthesizer-heavy techno-pop interpretations.

GOING GLOBAL

The music scene has changed rapidly with technology and its global transmission. In 2002, pop rock artist Kelly Clarkson won the first season of *American Idol*, a reality TV show that invites singers to compete for fame and a record deal with a major label. People all over the world vote after each show for favorites via text messaging, online, or with the *American Idol* app.

From 2008 to 2012, viral sensations including former busker Justin Bieber, "Call Me Maybe"s' Carly Rae Jepsen, and "Gangham Style"s' Psy and his horse dance experienced overnight international success. Today, instant access to downloads is our new normal. Listeners wear earbuds and toe-tap to personal playlists. We view music videos online and in our palms. We connect with artists through social networking, something unheard of not so long ago.

Not everyone is thrilled with the changes in ways we experience music. In 2011, rocker Jon Bon Jovi lamented the loss of a "magical, magical time." He told the U.K.'s *Sunday Times Magazine*, "Kids today have missed the whole experience of putting the headphones on, turning it up to 10, holding the jacket, closing their eyes and getting lost in an album; and the beauty of taking your allowance money and making a decision based on the jacket, not knowing what the record sounded like, and looking at a couple of pictures and still imagining it."

LONG AND WINDING ROAD

We've taken a long and winding road from *The Bay Psalm Book*, America's first book and first book of music. African traditions that collided and mingled with European ways of life in the New World spread deep and sprawling roots through many genres. They have stayed vibrantly alive in jazz and blues, rock, hip-hop, and more.

Part of our collective identity, all of this music reflects American history and heritage. Artists compose music to explore the time in which they live. From the sorrows of slave life to the unity of patriotism, from the struggles for equality and the soaring power of hope, these social, political, and religious influences shaped American life—and American sound.

Every generation faces change. But one thing remains the same. Music strikes a chord in its listeners. It has the power to touch emotions and stir the soul. It inspires action. It can overcome.

What's next in our musical evolution? Stay tuned. The times are always a-changin'.

Notable Quotable

"Hip-hop is the last true folk art."

—MC Mos Def (1973–)

SAY WHAT? MONDEGREEN GAME

Have you misheard a song's lyrics? There's a word for that—mondegreen! It's the misinterpretation or mishearing of a phrase, such as a line in a poem or a lyric in a song. American writer Sylvia Wright coined the term. She misheard a lyric in "The Bonny Earl O'Moray," a Scottish ballad. "Laid him on the green" became "Lady Mondegreen."

A mondegreen gives lyrics a whole new and often hilarious unintended meaning. Pop and rap songs are especially misheard. Why? It's usually more about the artist's enunciation than the listener's auditory acuity. And the songs are fast! With your classmates and friends, design a mondegreen game.

- **What are some questions to consider?** What mondegreens have you experienced? Listen to songs to focus on misheard lyrics. What do you think causes you to mishear?

MUSICAL NOTE

Gavin Edwards is the author of three books of mondegreens. One is *'Scuse Me While I Kiss This Guy.* Sound familiar? It's misheard from the 1967 Jimi Hendrix classic "Purple Haze." What's the actual lyric? "Excuse me while I kiss the sky."

On an online archive of misheard lyrics, listeners share slips of the ear. One person misheard Linkin Park's "In the End." "Keep that in mind that I designed this rhyme" became, "Keep that in mind that lasagna's rhyme."

- **Brainstorm some approaches your game might take to challenge the listener.** Will you use recorded music? Sing lyrics? Design an animated computer game? Perform a takeoff of a TV game show like *Jeopardy*?

- **Conceptualize your game on paper.** Set and explain the parameters. How many contestants can play simultaneously? What are the rules? How will you tally points?

- **When the game is ready, invite contestants to participate.** Afterward, assess and evaluate the game. What changes can you make to improve it?

To investigate more, go beyond your group to ask others to share misheard lyrics. Incorporate additional mondegreens into your game.

Do you ever get a song stuck in your head? There's a word for that phenomenon—earworm! It comes from a translation of the German word *Ohrwrum*. Try adding earworms to your game.

Dr. Victoria William studies music psychology. She explains that earworm "refers to the experience of having a tune or a part of a tune stuck in your head. Often a person experiencing an earworm has no idea why a tune has popped into their head and has little control over how long it continues." It's a common phenomenon affecting over 90 percent of the population at least once a week.

Ideas for Supplies ▼

- journal and pencil
- variety of music
- recording equipment
- computer

Notable Quotable

"(Taylor) Swift writes perfect pop songs that stick in your head like lollipops stuck in your hair."

—Journalist Nancy Jo Sales

**Inquire &
Investigate** ▶

BODY BEAT BOX

Beat boxing, which is wildly popular with rap artists, is a form of vocal percussion. Its long, creative history is a celebration of spontaneity that dates to juba dancing. Explore the different sounds you can produce with just your body.

- **Test some techniques to create sounds with your mouth.** Inhale and exhale as a percussive device to establish a beat. Explore your articulators. Click your tongue against your palate. What kinds of sounds can you make with your mouth and lips? Imitate the whines and trills of musical instruments with your voice. Change pitches as you whistle. Work with a microphone to amplify and layer sounds.

Notable Quotable

"The beautiful thing about hip-hop is it's like an audio collage. You can take any form of music and do it in a hip-hop way and it'll be a hip-hop song. That's the only music you can do that with."

—Talib Kweli, alternative rapper

- **Test body percussion.** Rub, clap, and slide your hands together. Flick your finger with your thumb. What percussive sounds can you produce by thumping your chest, slapping your thighs, and stomping your feet? Can you think of anything else?

- **Select tunes from your personal playlist with which to keep percussive time.** Improvise with the songs. Try freestyling along with the beats, or recite a piece of poetry to the rhythm. What sounds surprised you? Which techniques worked best?

- **Record yourself on garage band one "instrument" at a time.** Can you sound like a whole band just using your vocals and body?

To investigate more, watch and listen to the artists listed below. Then use your discoveries to choreograph a juba dance and perform your own beatbox song.

- DeStorm Power is an Internet sensation who tackles multiple genres with complex, layered beatbox covers. Watch his covers of Michael Jackson's "Beat It," Bon Jovi's "My Life," and the holiday classic, "Carol of the Bells." Work with your group to have everyone contribute to layers of beatboxing as you cover a song of your choice.

- Stomp is a group that performs choreographed percussion. Let their exuberant moves inspire your own choreography.

- Listen to the astonishing instrument-free covers from Texas a cappella band Penatonix. How do the artists mimic instruments?

Notable Quotable

"The music I'm listening to was recorded to studio tape long ago, pressed to vinyl, digitized onto my home computer decades later, uploaded to iTunes Match, and streamed through the cloud to my laptop. Kind of cool when you think about it."

—Eric P., Facebook post

SHOWTIME!

This book has introduced you to many genres of music. You've learned about the history behind the different styles, and the way that music expresses the feelings of people, confronts the issues of society, and helps us understand current events. Music is fun and makes you want to move!

Work with your classmates, friends, or family to create, rehearse, and perform a live musical show. Include some of the genres you've explored in this book.

- **Jot down ideas and let your creativity fly as you collaborate.** Decide where you'll perform the show and what kinds of acts and numbers you'll include in the lineup. Which music genres will you feature? What kind of dances will you choreograph? Which instruments will you play? What production numbers will bookend the show's opening and finale?

- **Discuss ways that you'll publicize the show.** How can you invite an audience?

- **It takes time to get the show ready for performance.** Develop a rehearsal schedule to allow all performers to adequately prepare. How can you work together to rehearse your numbers? How can you share suggestions for improvement? Help one another gather or make costume pieces.

- **How do you want your performing space to look?** Have some fun with decorations and sets if you choose to use them.

MUSICAL NOTE

Some actors and musicians are superstitious. It's bad luck to say, "Good luck!" Before going on stage, actors and musicians tell one another, "Break a leg!" The origins of the phrase are murky. Some people believe it means a performer will put on such a fantastic show that he or she will snap a leg, taking bow after bow.

- **Determine the running order of the numbers and acts.** Design a program to distribute to the audience. Title each number, and include the names of the performers in each.

- **Conduct a final dress rehearsal before you perform for an audience.**

- **On the stage, enjoy the fun of creativity.** Break a leg!

To investigate more, look up one of your favorite artists and watch a live show online. What did they do to engage their audience? Why did they choose to perform those particular songs?

a cappella: performed by voice only, without musical accompaniment.

abolitionist: a person supporting the end of slavery.

acoustic: music that is not electronically amplified.

acoustics: the scientific study of sound.

acuity: sharpness of hearing or sight.

African American: an American of African descent.

alliteration: the repetition of like sounds at the beginning of words in sequence.

alternative: a style of music that emerged in the late 1980s and early 1990s, which is characterized by bands with a do-it-yourself, non-conformist attitude.

alto: the second highest voice in a four-part chorus. It is typically the lowest female voice and the highest male voice.

amplify: to make a sound louder.

anonymous: not identified by name.

anthem: a song praising and declaring loyalty to something or a popular song that has become associated with a group, period, or cause that celebrates a sense of solidarity with it.

articulator: a moving or fixed organ involved in the sound-making process, including lips, tongue, teeth, and palate.

audible: loud or clear enough to be heard.

auditory: relating to hearing.

auditory nerve: the nerves that send impulses from the ear to the brain.

backbeat: a heavy, steady rhythm that stresses the second and fourth beats in a four-beat measure, often characteristic of rhythm and blues and other types of rock music.

ballad: poetic verses set to song.

balladeer: someone who performs ballads.

bar: a unit of time in music, divided according to the number of beats. Also called a measure.

baritone: a male voice with a range higher than a bass and lower than a tenor.

beat: an interval of measured time.

blues: a type of popular music that developed from African American folk songs in the early twentieth century. Its slow sad songs are performed over a repeating harmonic pattern.

boogie-woogie: a percussive blues piano playing in quadruple time, featuring improvisation.

Broadway: a group of theaters in the Times Square neighborhood of New York City that are considered to stage the highest level of theater in the country.

busker: a street performer.

casualty: someone killed or injured in battle.

center of gravity: the point at which gravity is concentrated.

civil rights: the basic rights that all citizens of a society are supposed to have, such as the right to vote.

Civil War (1861–1865): the war between the northern states and southern states that ended slavery and began the process of creating a more unified country.

civilian: someone not in the military.

cochlea: the spiral-shaped structure in the inner ear that sends signals to the auditory nerve.

collective identity: the characteristics of a group that make it unique.

colonial: relating to the years 1607 through 1776, when people from Europe settled in colonies in America. The colonial period ended when the Declaration of Independence was signed and the United States of America was formed.

commercial: relating to the buying and selling of goods or services, with the purpose of making money.

communism: a system of government in which a single party holds power and the state controls the economy.

composer: a person who writes music.

conductivity: the ability of an object or substance to transmit heat, electricity, or sound.

Confederate: refers to the group of southern slave states that seceded from the Union and formed their own government in 1861.

counterculture: a culture with values that run deliberately counter to the larger society.

country: popular music played on guitars and fiddles, based on traditional folk music from the South and cowboy music from the West. The songs express strong personal emotions.

cover: to record a new version of a song that was first sung or made popular by another performer.

cultural: relating to a culture or civilization, or to the arts.

culture: the beliefs and way of life of a group of people.

data: information, facts, and numbers.

decibel: a unit used to measure the loudness of a sound.

democracy: a government elected freely by the people.

digital: involving the use of computer technology.

disco: a style of pop music with a steady pronounced beat, popular in the 1970s for dancing. It developed from soul music, in response to the growing popularity of discos.

dissention: to disagree with a widely held opinion.

diversity: when many different people or things exist within a group or place.

DJ: a disc jockey, someone who plays recorded music.

download: to transfer data from one digital device to another.

eclectic: from a variety of sources or styles.

embellish: to add detail or decoration. In music, to add extra notes, accents, or trills to a melody to make it more beautiful or interesting.

embouchure: the mouthpiece of a wind instrument and the positioning of the lips, tongue, and facial muscles when playing an instrument.

emotion: a strong feeling about something or somebody.

enduring: long lasting.

enhance: to make greater.

escapism: entertainment that allows people to take a break from life's harsh realities.

ethnically: relating to a group of people who share a common national, racial, or religious background.

falsetto: a singing voice that extends higher than a singer's normal range.

field holler: an agricultural work song created during the slave era, which involved call-and-response patterns sung while working at a particular, often synchronized pace.

fife: a wooden, high-pitched flute commonly used in military and marching military groups.

flapper: a fashionable young woman in the 1920s who wore short skirts and a short hairstyle, listened to jazz, and often behaved in ways not considered acceptable at the time.

flourish: to add a special element to something.

flow: a total immersion in creative expression with no inhibitions or self-criticism.

folk: traditional, narrative songs that common people pass down in the oral tradition. Folk is a form of music that expresses the struggles of the time and in which everyone is welcome to participate.

folk rock: a musical genre combining elements of folk and rock music.

forbearance: patience and tolerance in a difficult situation.

force: a push or pull acted upon an object.

frequency: the number of sound waves that pass a specific point each second.

friction: the rubbing of one object against another.

funk: a popular music genre that derives from jazz, blues, and soul. It is characterized by a heavy rhythmic bass and backbeat.

garage rock: a type of music prevalent in the 1960s that was more aggressive than was common at the time, often with growled or shouted vocals that dissolved into incoherent screaming.

generation gap: the difference in attitudes, behavior, and interests between people of different generations, especially between parents and their children.

genre: a category of artistic work.

geographical: relating to the features of the land.

gospel: religious music.

gramophone: an antique record player.

graph: a diagram used to show the relationship between two quantities that vary.

gravity: a physical force that draws bodies toward the center of the earth.

griot: a wandering poet or storyteller in West Africa.

grunge: an alternative rock form of the 1980s and 1990s characterized by heavily distorted electric guitars and apathetic or angst-filled lyrics.

hard rock: a form of loud, aggressive rock music that emphasizes electric guitar used with distortion and other effects.

harmony: a pleasing blend of two or more tones.

heavy metal: a highly amplified, harsh-sounding rock music with a strong beat.

heritage: the art, buildings, traditions, and beliefs that are important to a country's or the world's history.

hip-hop: a form of popular culture originating in the African American inner city areas, characterized by rap music, graffiti art, and breakdancing.

hook: a musical idea that attracts attention and the listener's ear.

hymn: a religious song of praise and worship.

hypothesis: an unproven idea that tries to explain certain facts or observations.

iconic: describes something that is famous for or symbolizes an idea, group of things, or period of time.

identity: the characteristics that somebody recognizes as belonging uniquely to himself or herself, that describes individual personality for life.

illiterate: not able to read or write.

immigrate: to move to a foreign country to live there permanently. An immigrant is a person who immigrates.

improvisation: created and performed without preparation. Music composed, sung, and played without planning or rehearsal.

indentured: commited to serve a master or employer for free for a certain period of time, often to pay a debt.

independence: being in control of your own country, government, or actions.

indie: a small independent business, especially related to music or film.

individualism: the pursuit of personal happiness and independence rather than goals or interests of a group.

industrial: related to manufacturing.

inequality: differences in opportunity and treatment based on social, ethnic, racial, or economic qualities.

injustice: unfair treatment of someone.

inspirational: affecting your emotions or giving you the enthusiasm to do or create something.

instrumental: for musical instruments, not voices.

intensity: the strength, power, or force of something.

jazz: popular music that originated among African Americans in New Orleans in the late nineteenth century. It is characterized by syncopated rhythms and improvisation. Jazz originally drew on ragtime, gospel, black spiritual songs, West African rhythms, and European harmonies.

juba: a dance style created by slaves that is accompanied with rhythmic hand-clapping and thigh and knee slaps.

jump blues: uptempo blues featuring horns that was a forerunner of R&B.

kaleidoscopic: a changing form or pattern in a symmetrical way as it occurs in a kaleidoscope.

landlord: a property owner who rents out land or housing.

lip synch: to move your lips along with a recorded speech or song.

lyrics: the words to a song.

mainstream: the prevailing thoughts, influences, or activities of a society or a group.

martial: related to war, soldiers, and military life.

measure: a unit of time in music, divided according to the number of beats. Also called a bar.

megaphone: a funnel-shaped device used to direct and amplify the voice or other sound.

melancholy: feeling or making someone feel a thoughtful sadness.

melodramatic: dramatic, sentimental, and highly emotional.

metaphorical: using a word or phrase that normally means one thing to mean something else, such as "a sea of trouble".

meter: rhythmic lines of verse.

middle class: the section of society between the poor and the wealthy, including business and professional people and skilled workers.

migration: moving from one place to another.

mimic: to copy something.

minstrel: a traveling musician or an entertainer in a variety show.

molecule: a tiny particle that combines with other molecules to make up air, water, rocks, you—everything.

momentum: the speed or force of an object's forward movement.

monopoly: control by one company or party.

MP3: a computer file standard for downloading compressed music from the Internet.

muffle: to make a sound less loud or distinct.

music: a creative, artistic arrangement of sound.

narrative: a story or account of events.

national anthem: a patriotic song that honors the history, traditions, and struggles of its people, which is either recognized officially by the government or unofficially through use by the people.

national heritage: the art, buildings, traditions, and beliefs that are important to a country's history.

New World: the land now made up of North and South America. It was called the New World by people from Europe because it was new to them.

◂ GLOSSARY

noodle: to improvise on a musical instrument in a random way, often to warm up.

notes: arrangements of musical sounds in a specific order.

octave: the rhythmic grouping of eight tones, or the interval between the first and eighth tones on the musical scale.

oral tradition: passing stories, songs, and histories from one generation to another by mouth rather than in writing.

origin: the source of where something came from or where it began.

palate: the roof of the mouth.

parlor music: popular music played at home by members of the family.

patriotic: a feeling of devotion to and love for one's country.

patriotism: devotion to and love for one's country.

percussive: something that is hit.

perforate: to make a hole in something.

persecute: to cause harm or suffering to someone, often because of race or political beliefs.

phonograph: a machine that picks up and reproduces the sounds that have been recorded in the grooves cut into a vinyl record.

physics: the study of physical forces, including matter, energy, and motion.

physiology: the study of the internal workings of living things.

pinna: the external portion of the ear.

pitch: how high or low a sound is, depending on its frequency.

pop: modern commercial music, usually tuneful, uptempo and repetitive. Pop is aimed at the general public and the youth market in particular.

popular culture: cultural activities or commercial products reflecting or produced for the general masses of people.

precursor: something that comes before another of the same kind.

production number: a special musical routine performed by an entire cast, including singers, dancers, comics, etc.

prolific: producing many works.

protest: a statement or action expressing disapproval of or objection to something.

Psalm: a sacred song or poem of praise, especially from the Book of Psalms from the Bible.

punk rock: a fast, hard-edged music popular in the 1970s, typically with short songs, stripped-down instrumentation, and often political, anti-establishment lyrics.

R&B: rhythm and blues, a popular music style that combines jazz and blues with a strong backbeat.

racially: relating to race.

racist: hatred of people of a different race.

ragtime: a popular genre of the early 1900s, with a syncopated melody and an accompaniment of regular accents.

rap: spoken or chanted lyrics that rhyme, performed in time to a beat.

raspy: a rough, scratchy sound.

ration: limiting the amount of something to be used each week or month.

raucous: harsh and loud noise.

rebel: to fight against authority or someone fighting against authority.

rebellion: defying authority or an organized attempt to overthrow a government or other authority.

refrain: a line or group of lines repeated at the end of each verse. Also called the chorus.

reggae: Jamaican music featuring off-beat rhythmic accents.

resist: to refuse to do something.

resonance: the sound produced by a vibrating object.

reveille: a bugle call or trumpet call most often associated with the military. Mainly used to wake military personnel at sunrise.

Revolutionary War (1776–1783): the war between the colonies and the British government that ended with independence from England and the creation of the United States of America.

rhyme scheme: a pattern of rhyming lines in a poem. Letters such as a-b-c-a illustrate the way the lines rhyme.

rhythm: a regular pattern of beats in a musical piece.

riff: a repeated series of notes.

roadhouse: an inn, restaurant, or nightclub located on a road outside a town or city.

rock: a style of pop music, derived from rock and roll, usually played on electric or electronic instruments and equipment.

rock and roll: pop music derived from blues music that has heavily stressed beats. It is usually played on electric instruments and has simple, often repetitive, lyrics.

rockabilly: an early style of rock and roll music dating to the 1950s that combines elements of country, R&B, and bluegrass.

sacrifice: to give something up for the sake of something else.

salvation: deliverance from harm, ruin, or loss.

satirical: relating to literary wit that makes fun of people, their vices, and foolish behavior.

scale: a series of musical notes.

scat: a vocal improvisation common in jazz, often using only sounds and no words at all.

scratching: a DJ technique that involves producing sounds with vinyl records on turntables.

secular: not religious.

segregation: the practice of keeping racial, ethnic, or social groups separate.

sensation: a physical feeling.

self-expression: the communication of your own personality, feelings, or ideas, often through speech or art.

sharecropper: a farmer who works on someone else's land and receives a small share of a crop's value after paying for tools, seeds, housing, etc.

sinuses: cavities filled with air between the face and the skull.

social injustice: when people are treated unequally within a society.

society: an organized community of people.

soft rock: often derived from folk rock, using acoustic instruments and putting more emphasis on melody and harmonies.

soprano: the highest register of the female voice or a boy's voice.

soul: a combination of gospel and R&B music.

sound wave: invisible vibrations in the air that you hear as sound.

spiritual: a religious song arising from slavery that was inspired by the Old Testament of the Bible.

spontaneous: happening without planning.

stanza: a group of lines forming the basic recurring unit in a poem or song.

▾ GLOSSARY

stereotypical: an overly simplified image of a person or group.

superfluous: unnecessary, or more than enough.

symmetry: in mathematical terms, corresponding in size, shape, and positions on both sides of an axis. In artistic terms, beauty in form based on balance.

synchronize: to occur at the same time.

syncopated: a musical rhythm that puts a stress on beats that are usually not stressed.

synthesizer: a device that generates electronic music or modifies sounds electronically.

techno: electronic dance music with a quick tempo created by digitally synthesized instruments.

technology: tools, methods, and systems used to solve a problem or do work.

tempo: the pace at which a musical piece is played, typically indicated on a composition.

toasting: chanting or talking over a rhythmic beat.

tone: the specific quality of musical sound.

Top 40: the most popular songs each week.

transverse: a flute held horizontally, not vertically like a recorder.

tympanic membrane: the thin layer of connective tissue in the ear, commonly called the eardrum.

Underground Railroad: a secret network of safe houses and people who helped slaves escape from slavery in the South. The Underground Railroad brought people to the North and Canada where slavery was not legal in the years before the American Civil War.

Union: the term used for the federal (national) government of the United States in the Civil War, which also referred to the northern states.

universal: used or understood by everyone.

upbeat: cheerful.

uprising: an act of rebellion or revolt against authority.

uptempo: having a quick-moving tempo, or pace.

urban: relating to a city.

variation: a different version of an original poem or song.

vaudeville: wildly popular entertainment in the late nineteenth and early twentieth centuries, which featured a variety of comedy acts, singers, musicians, and dancers.

velocity: the speed at which something moves and in what direction.

vibrate: to move back and forth quickly.

vibration: a back-and-forth movement.

victory garden: a garden planted by American civilians during World War II. About 2 million victory gardens produced 40 percent of the food grown in the United States during the war.

Victrola: a popular brand of antique record player.

vocal cord: one of two membranes stretched across the larynx through which air passes in the process of making sound.

vocal range: the measure of the range of pitches your voice can make.

vinyl: plastic records played on phonographs.

vulgar: crude or obscene, or poorly behaved.

▾ RESOURCES

↳BOOKS

Record Store Days: From Vinyl to Digital and Back Again.
Calamar, Gary and Phil Gallo. Sterling, 2009.

Woodstock: Three Days That Rocked the World
Evans, Mike and Paul Kingsbury, eds. Sterling, 2009.

The Recording Secrets Behind 50 Great Albums.
Gorden, Kylee Swenson, ed. Back Beat Books, 2012.

Raggin', Jazzin', Rockin': A History of American Musical Instrument Makers.
VanHecke, Susan. Boyds Mills, 2011.

↳WEBSITES

American Treasures of the Library of Congress
www.loc.gov/exhibits/treasures/

John F. Kennedy Center for the Performing Arts
www.kennedy-center.org

Mariner's Museum: Captive Passage
http://marinersmuseum.org/sites/micro/captivepassage/index.html

Memphis Rock 'n' Soul Museum
http://memphisrocknsoul.org/

National Music Museum
http://orgs.usd.edu/nmm/galleries.html

Patriotic Melodies, the Library of Congress
http://lcweb2.loc.gov/diglib/ihas/html/patriotic/patriotic-home.html

Rock and Roll Hall of Fame
www.rockhall.com

Transatlantic Slave Trade Database:
http://slavevoyages.org/tast/index.faces

Turner Classic Movies:
www.tcm.com

▾ INDEX

A

acoustics, 6
activities
  Beat of the Drum, 31
  Become a Balladeer, 32–33
  Body Beat Box, 106–107
  Boogie Woogie Bugle, 76–77
  Changin' Times: Songs of
  Social Protest, 78–79
  Get Your Groove On! Gravity
  and Balance in Dance, 74–75
  'Gimme Fife!', 48–49
  Jug Band Acoustics, 52–53
  Kaleidoscopic Extravaganza,
  82–83
  Lift Every Voice and Sing,
  34–35
  Listen Up! Auditory Acuity,
  16–17
  A Map to Freedom, 36–37
  Oh, Say, Can You Sing?,
  50–51
  People Have the Power,
  92–93
  Pick a Sound, 64–65
  Pump Up the Volume, 18–19
  Rockin' Robin, 94–95
  Say What? Mondegreen
  Game, 104–105
  Showtime!, 108–109
  Sing in Harmony, 80–81
  Splish, Splash, 14–15
  Warbling Wineglasses, 12–13
American Bandstand, 87
Andrews Sisters, 70, 76
animals, music among, 10–11,
  94–95
Armstrong, Louis, vi, 58, 60
auditory acuity, 16–17, 104–105.
  See also hearing

B

Baez, Joan, vii, 25, 72, 79
ballads, 25, 32–33
banjos and guitars, vi, 2, 8, 9,
  26, 30, 51, 52, 58, 59, 61,
  63, 64–65, 91
"Battle Hymn of the Republic,"
  vi, vii, 44–45
The Bay Psalm Book, vi, 23, 103
Beach Boys, 8, 9, 10
beat boxing, 99, 106–107
The Beatles, vii, 73, 83, 89, 90
Berkeley, Busby, 82–83
Berry, Chuck, 86, 89
Beyoncé, 32, 51
Billboard charts, vi, vii, 73,
  86, 88
Blow, Kurtis, 100–101
"Blowin' in the Wind," vii, 78–79
bluegrass music, 29, 62, 63,
  64–65
blues music, 22, 57–58, 70, 72,
  86, 91
"Boogie Woogie Bugle Boy," vi,
  70, 76
British bands, vii, 90. *See also*
  The Beatles; The Rolling
  Stones; The Who
Broadway music, 69, 70–71,
  82–83
Brooks, Garth, 60, 62

C

Campbell, Clive, vii, 99
CDs and CD players, vii, 24, 101
civil rights movement, 69, 72, 78
Civil War, vi, 44–45
Cline, Patsy, 62, 63
Cohan, George M., vi, 47, 69
colonial-era music, 22–37
country and western music, vi,
  22, 60–63, 86, 88
cowboy music, 61, 62

D

dancing, vi, 11, 27, 30, 31,
  45–46, 56, 58, 60, 63, 69,
  71, 74–75, 82–83, 99
decibels, 7, 18–19
DJing, vii, 99, 100
DJ Kool Herc, vii, 99
drums, vi, 8, 27, 30, 31, 42, 51, 58
Dylan, Bob, vii, 72, 78–79, 87

E

ears, human, 7–8, 14–15, 16–17
Edison, Thomas, vi
The Ed Sullivan Show, vii, 89, 90
Eminem, 98, 100

F

fiddles, 57, 61, 63, 64
folk music, 3, 22, 24–25, 29,
  32–33, 88
folk rock music, 86, 87
"Follow the Drinking Gourd,"
  28–29, 36–37
The Four Tops, 73, 80
Frizzell, Lefty, 62, 63

G

Gaye, Marvin, 73, 79
"Good Vibrations," 8, 9, 10
gospel music. *See* spirituals and
  religious music
Grand Ole Opry, vi, 61
guitars. *See* banjos and guitars

H

Haley, Bill and the Comets,
  vii, 88, 89
hearing, 7–8, 14–15, 16–17,
  104–105
heavy metal music, 86, 87, 91
Hendrix, Jimi, 51, 72, 104
hip-hop music, vii, 22, 98–101,
  103, 104, 106–107
honky-tonk music, 62, 63
Howe, Julia Ward, vi, 45

I

indie music, 90, 91
instruments, vi, 2, 8, 9, 12–13, 26, 27, 30, 31, 42, 48–49, 51, 52–53, 57–58, 61, 62–63, 64–65, 70, 76–77, 91, 102, 106–107
Internet, music via, vii, 4, 86, 101, 102, 107
iPods, vii, 4
iTunes, vii, 101, 107

J

Jackson, Michael/Jackson 5, vii, 73, 95
Jay Z, 98, 100
jazz music, vi, 22, 56–57, 58–60, 63, 72
"John Brown's Body," 44–45
Joplin, Janis, 59, 60, 72, 90
juba rhythms, vi, 30, 31, 57, 106–107

K

Key, Francis Scott, vi, 43
King, Martin Luther, Jr., 72, 79
Korean War, 68

L

Led Zeppelin, 87, 91
"Lift Every Voice and Sing," 34, 35
Little Richard, 86, 89
live street performances, 100
loudness and intensity of sound, 7, 14–15, 18–19, 35

M

The Marvelettes, 73, 80
McGraw, Tim, 60, 62
minstrel shows, 45, 46, 70
Motown, 73, 80
MP3s, 4, 31, 101
MTV, vii, 101

music
art and science of, 3–4
bluegrass music as, 29, 62, 63, 64–65
blues music as, 22, 57–58, 70, 72, 86, 91
Broadway music or musicals as, 69, 70–71, 82–83, 108–109
colonial-era music as, 22–37
country and western music as, vi, 22, 60–63, 86, 88
cowboy music as, 61, 62
dancing to, vi, 11, 27, 30, 31, 45–46, 56, 58, 60, 63, 69, 71, 74–75, 82–83, 99
folk music as, 3, 22, 24–25, 29, 32–33, 88
hip-hop music as, vii, 22, 98–101, 103, 104,106–107
honky-tonk music as, 62, 63
influences on, 2–3, 22–23, 86
instruments for playing, vi, 2, 8, 9, 12–13, 26, 27, 30, 31, 42, 48–49, 51, 52–53, 57–58, 61, 62–63, 64–65, 70, 76–77, 91, 102, 106–107
jazz music as, vi, 22, 56–57, 58–60, 63, 72
minstrel shows including, 45, 46, 70
Motown Sound in, 73, 80
Native American music as, 31
patriotic music as, 40–53, 68, 69, 71
personal preferences in, 2, 4, 8
playlists of, 2, 10, 11, 25, 27, 29, 30, 32, 34, 41, 45, 57, 58, 59, 60, 62, 70, 80, 87, 88, 90, 92, 101
pop music as, 3, 32, 70, 104–105
protest music as, vii, 68–69, 71–72, 78–79, 91, 92–93
rap music as, vii, 99, 100–101, 104, 106–107
R&B music as, vi, 22, 50, 80, 86, 88, 95
Roaring Twenties music as, 56–65
rock and roll as, vi–vii, 3, 8, 15, 59, 73, 86–95
singing, 34–35, 50–51, 80–81
slavery and slave music as, vi, 22–23, 25–31, 34–37, 44–45, 57–58, 61, 64, 78, 100
spirituals and religious music as, vi, 22, 23, 27–28, 34, 58, 69, 78, 86, 88
technology influencing, vii, 4, 86, 98–109 (see also radio; televised music)
timeline of, vi–vii
vaudeville entertainment including, vi, 45–46, 52, 70
vibrations creating, 6–19, 34–35, 48, 52, 64
wartime music as, vi, vii, 40–53, 68, 69–70, 71–72, 74, 78, 91, 101
written/music notation/sheet music, 10, 46, 47, 102
musicals, 69, 70–71, 82–83, 108–109
"My Girl," 73, 81

N

Nashville Sound, 63
national anthem, vi, 43, 50–51. See also "The Star-Spangled Banner"
Native American music, 31
noise, 8, 11
notes, 9, 10

O

"Over There," vi, 47

P

Pandora Radio, vii, 101
patriotic music, 40–53, 68, 69, 71
phonographs and records, vi, vii, 2, 4, 56, 61, 73, 80, 87, 88, 91, 99–100, 101, 107
"Piece of My Heart," 59, 90
pitch, 6, 8, 9–10, 35, 48, 53, 81, 94
playlists, 2, 10, 11, 25, 27, 29, 30, 32, 34, 41, 45, 57, 58, 59, 60, 62, 70, 80, 87, 88, 90, 92, 101
pop music, 3, 32, 70, 104–105
Presley, Elvis, vii, 86, 87, 88–89
protest music, vii, 68–69, 71–72, 78–79, 91, 92–93
punk rock music, 86, 87, 91

R

radio, vi, 4, 56, 61, 69, 86, 87
The Ramones, 87, 91
rap music, vii, 99, 100–101, 104, 106–107
R&B music, vi, 22, 50, 80, 86, 88, 95
records. See phonographs and records
religious music. See spirituals and religious music
resonance, 34
Revolutionary War, vi, 40–41, 48, 70
rhythm, 8, 10–11. See also juba rhythms; R&B music
Roaring Twenties music, 56–65
rock and roll, vi–vii, 3, 8, 15, 59, 73, 86–95
"Rock Around the Clock," vii, 88
Rolling Stone magazine, 59, 78, 90

The Rolling Stones, 59, 89, 90
Ross, Diana, 73, 80

S

Scruggs, Earl, 62, 65
Seeger, Pete, 25, 63, 71, 72, 79, 92
sheet music, 10, 46, 47, 102
Show Boat, 70, 71
singing, 34–35, 50–51, 80–81
slavery and slave music, vi, 22–23, 25–31, 34–37, 44–45, 57–58, 61, 64, 78, 100
Smith, Bessie, vi, 57, 59, 60
Smith, Patti, 91, 92
sound and sound waves, 6–8, 14–15, 18–19, 34–35
spirituals and religious music, vi, 22, 23, 27–28, 34, 58, 69, 78, 86, 88
Springsteen, Bruce, 71, 92, 101
"The Star-Spangled Banner," vi, 40, 42–43, 44, 50–51
Stomp, 30, 107
The Supremes, Diana Ross and, 73, 80
Swift, Taylor, 32, 50, 60, 62, 105

T

technology, vii, 4, 86, 98–109. See also radio; televised music
televised music, vii, 3, 87, 88, 89, 90, 101, 102
The Temptations, 73, 80–81
theater. See minstrel shows; musicals; vaudeville entertainment
tone, 9, 53

U

U2, 91, 92, 93
Underground Railroad, 28–29, 36–37

V

vaudeville entertainment, vi, 45–46, 52, 70
vibrations, 6–19, 34–35, 48, 52, 64
Vietnam War, 68, 71–72, 78, 91
volume. See loudness and intensity of sound

W

Walker, Kurt, 100–101
War of 1812, 42–43
wartime music, vi, vii, 40–53, 68, 69–70, 71–72, 74, 78, 91, 101
Waters, Muddy, 59
"We Shall Overcome," vii, 72, 79
The Who, 72, 87, 90
Williams, Hank, 62, 63
Wonder, Stevie, 73, 80
Woodstock Art & Music Fair, vii, 51, 72
World Trade Center attacks, vii, 44, 101
World War I, vi, 46–47
World War II, vi, 68, 69–70, 71, 74

Y

"Yankee Doodle," vi, 40, 41, 42